Pub Strolls in
KENT

Michael Easterbrook

COUNTRYSIDE BOOKS
NEWBURY BERKSHIRE

First published 2002
© Michael Easterbrook 2002

COUNTRYSIDE BOOKS
3 Catherine Road
Newbury, Berkshire

To view our complete range of books,
please visit us at
www.countrysidebooks.co.uk

ISBN 1 85306 725 3

For Val, Cheryl, Jolene and Craig

Produced through MRM Associates Ltd., Reading
Printed in Italy

Contents

AREA MAP SHOWING LOCATION OF THE WALKS

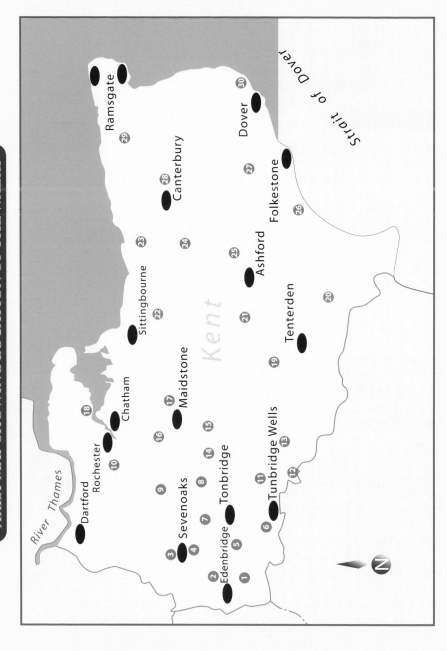

River Thames

Dartford

Rochester

Chatham

Maidstone

Sevenoaks

Edenbridge

Tonbridge

Tunbridge Wells

Sittingbourne

Kent

Ashford

Tenterden

Canterbury

Ramsgate

Dover

Folkestone

Strait of Dover

N

PUBLISHER'S NOTE

We hope that you obtain considerable enjoyment from this book; great care has been taken in its preparation. Although at the time of publication all routes followed public rights of way or permitted paths, diversion orders can be made and permissions withdrawn.

We cannot, of course, be held responsible for such diversion orders and any inaccuracies in the text which result from these or any other changes to the routes nor any damage which might result from walkers trespassing on private property. We are anxious though that all details covering the walks are kept up to date and would therefore welcome information from readers which would be relevant to future editions.

The simple sketch maps that accompany the walk in this book are based on notes made by the author whilst checking out the routes on the ground. However, for the benefit of a proper map, we do recommend that you purchase the relevant Ordnance Survey sheet covering your walk. The Ordnance Survey maps are widely available, especially through booksellers and local newsagents.

Kent is a large and lovely county. And can you think of one with more romantic and beautiful countryside? With its fruit orchards a froth of creamy white and pink blossom in spring and burnished with red and gold as the leaves change colour in autumn, it can still lay claim to being the 'Garden of England'. Several walks in this book provide the opportunity to see this display, such as the ones from Linton and Hernhill. Although the hop industry in Kent has been in decline for some time, it has left its legacy of oasthouses. Once used for drying hops, many have been converted into attractive places to live, and their round buildings and white cowls help to provide a distinctive rural landscape.

Kent also has the springy turf of the North Downs, complete with colourful arrays of wild flowers, including rare orchids, which thrive on the chalky soil. Flowers and butterflies abound on the walks from Thurnham and Trottiscliffe, and other walks, such as the ones from Otford, Chilham and Wye provide lovely views of the Downs. The heavily wooded Greensand Ridge running across the county, provides wonderful views over the lower ground of the Weald, as seen from the walks at Ide Hill and Shipbourne. The Weald has clay soils, and these provide ideal conditions for the sea of bluebells that colour its woods in the spring. The walks from Biddenden, Goudhurst and Lamberhurst, amongst others, are in this area. In contrast, there is the flat and mysterious landscape of Romney Marsh, viewed on the Appledore walk.

There are plenty of stately homes, gardens and castles to visit and more hidden delights tucked away in some of the small villages, where you come across medieval hall houses and typical Wealden weatherboarded cottages. Many of these historic jewels can be seen on the routes, such as those from Penshurst, Shipbourne and Godden Green.

Each stroll in the book is an easy, short, circular walk, with the added bonus of a friendly pub that offers, above all, excellent food as well as good ales. I have given brief details of the menus, including bar snacks, and also a telephone number in case you want to check opening times before your visit. If you wish to leave your car in the pub car park while you walk (patrons only, of course) please have a word with the landlord first. Alternatively, if you opt for roadside parking, do be careful not to block any entrances or exits.

These strolls vary in length from 1 mile to 4½ miles (although most are under 3 miles) and are all easily undertaken by family groups and the not-so-fit as well as those who walk regularly. They make use of rights of way and quiet lanes. Kent has its fair share of hills so be prepared for some gradual climbs – usually with a fine view as a reward. Finally, you will inevitably encounter muddy patches, even in dry weather, so it is wise to wear strong shoes or boots.

I hope you enjoy my selection of walks across the county, that you perhaps see places new to you, and that you have some good meals. Happy Strolling!

Michael Easterbrook

Hever
The King Henry VIII

DIRECTIONS TO START: HEVER IS 2 MILES SOUTH-EAST OF EDENBRIDGE AND CAN BE REACHED BY A MINOR ROAD FROM THE B2026 AT EDENBRIDGE OR FROM THE B2027 AT BOUGH BEECH. **PARKING:** IN THE CAR PARK OPPOSITE THE PUB, BUT ASK PERMISSION FIRST.

Although you may be lucky enough to see jousting knights on this walk, you haven't really stepped back in time, you will just be observing one of the special events in the grounds of historic Hever Castle, once the home of Anne Boleyn. What you are more certain of seeing as you stroll is some glorious countryside in the heart of the Weald. There are lovely views to distant hills and sections past mature woodland, with flowers, birds and other creatures to spot.

The King Henry VIII

Henry was a frequent visitor to this area when he was courting Anne Boleyn, and the pub that now bears his name is very popular with visitors who follow in his footsteps to Hever Castle. It has comfortable bars and eating areas, with beams, large fireplaces and wooden panelling providing an atmosphere of history. This is very appropriate, as there has been an inn here since 1597. Outside there is a lovely large garden with a pond and patio seating area. Shepherd Neame beers like Master Brew and Spitfire are on offer, as are Oranjeboom and Hurlimann lagers. A good choice of food is available, augmented by daily specials, for example tarragon cream chicken, vegetarian lasagne and quiche. There are also tempting desserts such as caramel apple pie, chocolate fudge cake and summer fruits pudding.

Opening times are 11.30 am to 3 pm and 6 pm to 11 pm, and food is served from 12 noon to 2 pm and 7 pm to 9 pm (not on Monday evening). Telephone: 01732 862457

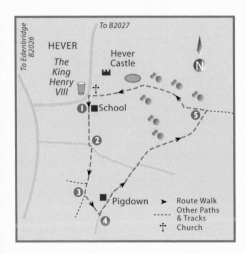

The Walk

① From the pub itself, cross the road with extreme care on the bend, and go down the drive to the left of the car park, past the school. The drive becomes a path, which continues with a wood to the left.

② On reaching a minor road go left, then after 60 yards go right up a bank at a footpath sign. Keep to the left edge of a field, with fine views back to the right, and through a gap in the hedge at the far left corner. Keep straight on across the next field and over two stiles in quick succession, then along the left edge of another field.

③ After 100 yards go left over a stile, shortly over another, then diagonally right up the field, aiming for the right corner of a wooden picket fence. At the top of the field, look back for a lovely view then go over a stile to a minor road.

④ Go left for ¼ mile, then just past where Rectory Lane goes off on the left, and the road bends right, go straight on at a stile next to a metal gate. Keep to the left edge of three fields, then continue on a path between a wood on the right and wire fence on the left.

⑤ The path emerges onto a metalled track by houses. The track has a gate with a 'Private Road' sign, so to get onto it go right for 10 yards, then left for 10 yards, to go left through a wooden gate with an Eden Valley Walk marker. Walk along the

Near Hever

tarmac private road, with woodland on your right, and 150 yards after it bends right go off the road at a marker post on the right. The path goes away from the road through trees, then crosses it by a wooden bridge, before skirting the grounds of Hever Castle between fences. Unfortunately, the castle is hidden by trees, but there are glimpses of the lake. The path eventually goes through the churchyard at Hever to reach the road, with the inn opposite.

PLACES OF INTEREST NEARBY

Hever Castle and Gardens – romantic castle with moat, and with impressive furniture and paintings. There are Italian, rose and Tudor gardens with a maze and lake. Open daily from March to November. Telephone 01732 865224.

Ide Hill
The Cock

MAP: OS EXPLORER 147 (GR 487518) | **WALK 2** | **DISTANCE:** 1½ OR 2¼ MILES

DIRECTIONS TO START: IDE HILL IS REACHED BY MINOR ROADS FROM THE A25 AT SUNDRIDGE, NEAR JUNCTION 5 OF THE M25. COMING FROM THE NORTH, THE PUB IS ON THE LEFT AFTER THE ROAD BENDS LEFT PAST THE VILLAGE GREEN.
PARKING: IN THE CAR PARK BEHIND THE PUB, WITH PERMISSION, OR, WITH CARE, AROUND THE VILLAGE GREEN.

The area around Ide Hill is a wonderful place for walking. The Greensand Ridge is heavily wooded and there are glorious views over the Weald. The beauty of the landscape was recognised by the National Trust, who own large amounts of land nearby. In spring bluebells and other colourful spring flowers abound, while in autumn the trees have beautiful gold and russet tints. The village has a large green and a tea and gift shop, in addition to a fine inn.

This stroll is made up of two short circuits, north and south of the pub, which can easily be combined (total distance 2¼ miles).

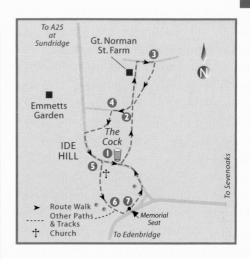

The Cock

This is the oldest building on the attractive village green of Ide Hill, dating back to at least 1755. At one time it was home to teams of heavy horses that were required to haul loaded wagons up one of the nearby hills, and until the beginning of the 20th century it was used for meetings of the Court Baron. These days it is host to gatherings of a convivial nature, providing a good choice of food and drink to help them along. Greene King IPA and Abbot Ale are available, as well as Scrumpy Jack cider, various lagers and a range of wines. The main menu includes steaks, scampi, gammon and salads, together with specials such as spicy sausage casserole and steak, pigeon and mushroom pudding at lunchtime and pheasant in white wine in the evening. There are some splendid desserts too, among them spotted dick, treacle tart and strawberry pavlova.

The pub is open from 11.30 am to 2.30 pm and 6 pm to 11 pm on Monday to Saturday and 12 noon to 3 pm and 7 pm to 10.30 pm on Sunday, with food served from 12 noon to 2 pm and 6 pm to 8.30 pm. Telephone: 01732 750310.

The Walk

① Going out of the pub, turn sharp left along the narrow road, marked as a cul-de-sac, in front of houses. At its end take the footpath signposted to Brook Place. The path goes slightly right across a field with fine views ahead to the North Downs. Cross a stile in the far right corner and turn left for a few yards to a lane.

② Turn right along the lane and on reaching a T-junction with another lane turn right.

③ After 200 yards cross a stile on the right opposite a drive. Keep to the right edge of fields, then between a fence and hedge, then diagonally left across a field and left of a house to emerge on the lane you were on earlier, where you go straight on.

④ Go left at a stile after 200 yards, diagonally right across a field to a gap in a hedge, then slightly right on a grassy track to a road. Turn left to return to the village and on reaching the green turn left to the pub.

⑤ To do the optional extra loop go straight on along the narrow road to the right of the village green then take the drive to the right of the church. Opposite the Old Vicarage a footpath leaves the drive on the right by a National Trust information board.

The Weald from Ide Hill

⑥ Just before the path opens out into a grassy clearing, take a path on the left at a Greensand Way (GSW) marker post. Follow it through trees to a T-junction with another path and turn left to a memorial seat to Octavia Hill, a founder of the National Trust. There is a stunning view from here.

⑦ Go past the back of the seat and straight on at the next GSW post and continue with a road below you through the trees on the right. At the next GSW post, by an information board, go left, then along the left edge of a grassy area with views back over Bough Beech Reservoir. The path goes down to a road. Turn left along the road (take extreme care – no footpath) for a short distance to return to the village green and the pub.

PLACES OF INTEREST NEARBY

Chartwell (National Trust), the family home of Sir Winston Churchill, is to the west of Ide Hill, off the B2026 south of Westerham. It is open from April to October, Wednesday to Sunday, plus Tuesdays in July and August. Telephone: 01732 866368. **Emmetts Garden** (National Trust) has rare trees and shrubs and colourful azaleas, rhododendrons and bluebells in spring. Open Wednesday to Sunday in April and May and Wednesday plus weekends from June to October. Telephone: 01732 868381.

Otford
The Horns

MAP: OS EXPLORER 147 (GR 526594)   **WALK 3**   DISTANCE: 2½ MILES

DIRECTIONS TO START: OTFORD IS ON THE A225, SOME 3 MILES NORTH OF
SEVENOAKS. THERE IS A RAILWAY STATION TO THE EAST OF THE VILLAGE.
PARKING: TO REACH THE LARGE PUBLIC CAR PARK, OR THE CAR PARK FOR
PATRONS BEHIND THE PUB, TURN OFF THE A225 BY THE DUCKPOND INTO THE
MAIN VILLAGE STREET. BOTH ARE ON THE RIGHT.

Otford is a large but attractive village which has several historic buildings including the remains of a 16th century archbishop's palace and an 11th century church, antiques and crafts shops, and the only duckpond that is scheduled as a listed building! The walk takes us through the enchanting landscape of the Darent valley, where the famous 19th century landscape painter Samuel Palmer found 'the nooks and dells of Paradise'. He lived in Shoreham, another lovely village nearby. Part of the walk goes alongside the river, which is tranquil and tree-lined for much of this stretch. If you are lucky you may spot a heron or even a flash of blue as a kingfisher skims by. The river has made a gap in the North Downs, and these hills provide lovely views along the walk at all times of year, but are particularly beautiful in autumn as the leaves turn to gold and bronze.

The Horns

This pub, which has a pretty tile-hung exterior, was formerly three cottages, and the modern alterations hide a timber-framed structure of the 16th or 17th century. The attractive dining areas feature these timbers, and from the windows at the front of the pub a magnificent medieval open-hall house can be seen across the street.

There is an extensive menu, including smoked salmon and prawns, rib of beef and ratatouille. There are also daily specials, which on the day I visited included wing of skate fillets and asparagus, bacon and mushrooms in a cheese sauce. Lighter meals such as omelettes are available, as are ploughman's lunches and a range of tasty baguettes and sandwiches. Beers available include Greene King IPA and Adnams.

Opening hours are 11 am to 2.30 pm and 6 pm to 11 pm on Monday to Friday, 11 am to 2.30 pm and 6.30 pm to 11 pm on Saturday and 12 noon to 3 pm and 7 pm to 10.30 pm on Sunday. Food is served 12 noon to 2 pm and 6.30 pm to 10 pm Monday to Saturday and on Sunday lunchtimes only, 12 noon to 3 pm. Telephone: 01959 522604.

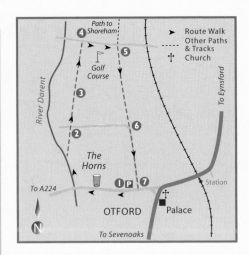

The Walk

① From the public car park turn right, after 250 yards passing the Horns on the right, which is the alternative starting point. Leave the main street by turning right at a sign for the Darent Valley Path (DVP) up a private drive alongside the river Darent. Once past houses and allotments go through a kissing gate then along the left edge of a field with the river on the left. Majestic dragonflies patrol the banks in summer. After 400 yards cross a stile and go straight across another field, keeping to the left edge with a fence on the left.

② At the next stile go straight across, ignoring a footpath sign pointing right, and over another stile after 20 yards. Continue along the right edge of the next field, with a tall hedge on an ancient boundary bank on the right. There are fine views of the valley ahead and to the left, and in the distance a white cross can be seen on the hills above Shoreham, cut out of the chalk as a memorial to those who died in the World Wars.

③ After 400 yards go over a stile and continue straight on with wire fences and hedges on both sides through a golf course. All of the hedges on this walk contain a wide range of trees and shrubs. The blossoms look lovely in spring, and in autumn there are lots of different fruits and berries.

The medieval hall house in Otford

④ After about ½ mile you reach wooden posts on the path. Turn right here along a narrow lane. Follow this lane for about 400 yards, and where there are entrances to the golf course to left and right (both with green metal gates) and the DVP path goes off to the left, take the path to the right instead.

⑤ The path goes between wire fences with hedges. Keep straight on as the golf course ends, now with a field on the left and a hedge on the right, until you reach a wooden gate.

⑥ Go through the gate onto another lane and continue straight ahead down the lane for ¾ mile, in the last section past farm buildings and houses and with a sports field on the right. This lane is believed to have been part of a Roman country road linking settlements in the valley.

⑦ On reaching the main street in Otford turn right to return to the village car park or the Horns.

PLACES OF INTEREST NEARBY

Lullingstone Castle, to the north of Shoreham, is a Tudor manor house with an impressive 16th century gatehouse. It is open on weekends from April to September. Telephone: 01322 862114. Nearby **Lullingstone Roman Villa** shows extensive excavations, with fine mosaics and a bathhouse. Protected under cover by English Heritage, it is open daily. Telephone: 01322 863467.

Godden Green
The Buck's Head

MAP: OS EXPLORER 147 (GR 553552)   WALK 4   DISTANCE: 2½ MILES

DIRECTIONS TO START: GODDEN GREEN IS 1½ MILES EAST OF SEVENOAKS, REACHED BY A MINOR ROAD FROM THE A25 AT SEAL, WITH THE PUB ON THE RIGHT, OPPOSITE THE VILLAGE GREEN. **PARKING:** AT THE PUB, WITH PERMISSION. THE WALK COULD ALSO BE STARTED FROM THE CAR PARK AT KNOLE HOUSE, POINT 4, OPEN WHEN THE HOUSE IS (SMALL CHARGE).

This walk goes past one of the finest historic houses in England, Knole House. Dating mainly from the 16th and early 17th century, the massive mansion has 365 rooms and 7 courtyards! You also go through the glorious parkland surrounding it, where you will see herds of deer, and trees that are hundreds of years old. There is lovely scenery and plenty of interesting wildlife such as woodpeckers and other woodland birds.

The Buck's Head

This friendly pub, in the hamlet of Godden Green on the edge of Knole Park, has roomy bars, a separate eating area and a pleasant garden at the rear. It serves a range of Shepherd Neame ales, including Spitfire, Goldings and Bishop's Finger, in addition to Oranjeboom lager. There is also an extensive wine list to accompany the food, which includes roast meats, plaice stuffed with prawns and mushrooms in white wine, and vegetarian meals such as cream cheese and broccoli bake. The range of hunger-busting pies, for example rabbit, beef and ale, chicken bacon and leek, and vegetable and herb is very popular too. Bar snacks include steak and kidney pudding, calamari, ploughman's lunches and filled jacket potatoes. There are mouth-watering desserts to follow and puddings are featured in winter – with steamed jam, sticky toffee and spotted dick among those on offer. The pub is open 12 noon to 3 pm and 5.30 pm to 11 pm Monday to Saturday and from 12 noon to 3 pm and 7 pm to 10.30 pm on Sunday. Food is served from 11.30 am to 2.30 pm and 6.45 pm to 9.30 pm (not Sunday and Monday evenings). Telephone 01732 761330.

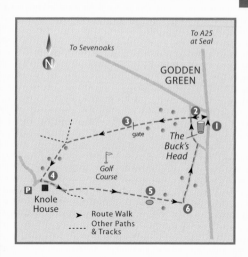

The Walk

① Going out of the pub turn left to walk in front of a row of houses, then turn left along a gravel drive, soon passing stables on the right.

② Go through a gateway and straight across a track to a footpath between bungalows. Where the path joins a wider, sandy track bear left. The track goes between trees, with lots of mauve rhododendron flowers providing colour in May and June.

③ Enter Knole Park Estate through a metal kissing gate next to a wooden gate, and keep on the tarmac track. Your first view of Knole House is in the distance on the left. The track goes gradually downhill and crosses a golf fairway (take care) to reach an avenue of oak trees, known as the Duchess Walk. You go gently uphill between the rows of trees to reach Knole House. If you need further refreshment there is a tea shop here (see Places of Interest Nearby).

④ If not visiting Knole, turn left at the end of the avenue of trees to go along the road alongside the house. Where the road narrows to a metalled track go diagonally left at the large oak tree with a yellow direction arrow on the trunk. Cross more

Impressive Knole House

golf fairways with care, but notice the fine views across to the North Downs on the left. Go past the 14th tee, then straight across a metalled track and through a clump of trees. The path continues across a small valley, then to the right of a dead tree, which is pocked with holes made by insects and woodpeckers.

⑤ Go past a small pond on the right, then keep to the left side of a small open area and between two tall trees at its end. Leave the Knole Estate 40 yards past these trees through a pedestrian gate and continue gently downhill to a stone house.

⑥ Turn left on the narrow road here and follow it for 600 yards to a T-junction, then go left on a narrower track between tall hedges. Follow it for 300 yards to cottages and the path on the right next to stables at point 2. Turn right here to return to the pub.

PLACES OF INTEREST NEARBY

Knole House (National Trust) is one of the largest mansions in Britain, with important collections of paintings, furniture and silver. Open from April to October, Wednesday to Sunday and Bank Holiday Mondays; deer park open daily throughout the year for pedestrians. Telephone: 01732 450608.

Penshurst
The Leicester Arms

MAP: OS EXPLORER 147 (GR 527437) | **WALK 5** | **DISTANCE:** 2¾ MILES

DIRECTIONS TO START: PENSHURST IS 4 MILES NORTH-WEST OF TUNBRIDGE WELLS, AT THE JUNCTION OF THE B2176, WHICH LEAVES THE A26 AT SOUTHBOROUGH, AND THE B2188, WHICH GOES NORTH FROM THE A264 NEAR LANGTON GREEN.
PARKING: IN THE CAR PARK AT THE REAR OF THE PUB, WITH PERMISSION.

A sense of history pervades the village of Penshurst, dominated as it is by the mansion of Penshurst Place. The walk provides fine views of the house, and also of the church and other old buildings, as well as offering tremendous views over the lovely wooded countryside around the village. Its many attributes make Penshurst popular with tourists, who are provided for by two tea shops, as well as an ancient inn.

The Leicester Arms

The long history of this 16th century coaching inn is evident in the interior, which has many beams, large inglenook fireplaces, and even some windows with stained glass. The dark wooden furniture fits well with these surroundings. There is plenty of room in the bar, also a separate restaurant and a terrace at the rear with seats providing good views. The restaurant has starters such as crispy coated whitebait and Stilton fritters, followed by steaks, rack of lamb, duck in honey and thyme jus, lemon sole filled with scallops and crab and vegetarian selections such as spinach, ricotta and goat's cheese cannelloni. In the bar there are daily specials like red Thai curry, tuna loin on Mediterranean vegetables or supreme of chicken filled with haggis with a whisky and mushroom cream sauce, as well as baguettes, ploughman's lunches and jacket potatoes. A good choice of ales is offered with Bass, Boddingtons, Adnams and Fuller's London Pride available, in addition to Scrumpy Jack cider and Heineken and Stella Artois lagers.

The inn is open, with bar food available, all day, and restaurant meals are served from 12 noon to 2.30 pm and from 7 in the evening. Telephone: 01892 870551.

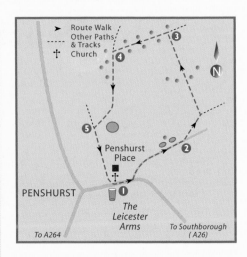

The Walk

① Cross the road from the front of the inn and follow it right to a bend. Here go left through an unusual stile with a walled arch next to the gate into Penshurst Place. Keep on the estate road, with the walled garden of the mansion on your left, then car parks, and continue past two large ponds. For most of the walk you are following a Penshurst Place Estate Trail.

② Just past the second pond, go left off the road at a stile by a metal gate and sharp right for 80 yards along a field edge to another stile. Go diagonally left up a field, past a marker post, pausing for a great view back over the mansion and church. Near the top of the field, turn left 20 yards before the hedge to walk between two rows of trees (some new) to a stile. Keep straight on along an earthen farm track, through a small wood, then up the right side of a field.

③ At the top of the field you reach a wide grassy track, running at right angles to you between two rows of plane trees. Turn left here at a marker post and continue along the avenue of trees, with woods on the right and glorious open views to the left, for 600 yards.

Penshurst Place dates back to the 14th century

④ Just past where the tree avenue ends, go diagonally left at a marker post and downhill between more lines of trees, this time mainly beech. About 250 yards before the end of the avenue of older trees and with a lake ahead, go diagonally right to a stile next to a metal gate. Keep to the left edge of a field with a fence on the left and where the fence bends away left keep straight on for 150 yards to a stile in a fence.

⑤ Go left over the stile and on towards Penshurst Place, with old oak trees on your left. Keep to the right of a cricket pitch, over an estate road, and past the mansion. At the end of its boundary hedge turn left into the churchyard and continue through its lychgate to return to the inn opposite.

PLACES OF INTEREST NEARBY
Penshurst Place dates back to the 14th century and has a unique medieval Baron's Hall, magnificent staterooms, and beautiful Tudor gardens as well as an adventure playground, shop and restaurant. Open daily from April to October and at weekends in March. Telephone: 01892 870307.

Speldhurst
The George & Dragon

MAP: OS EXPLORER 147 (GR 554414)   **WALK 6**   **DISTANCE:** 2¾ MILES

DIRECTIONS TO START: SPELDHURST IS 2 MILES NORTH-WEST OF TUNBRIDGE WELLS, REACHED BY MINOR ROADS FROM THE A264 AT LANGTON GREEN OR THE A26 AT SOUTHBOROUGH. THE INN IS OPPOSITE THE CHURCH. **PARKING:** IN THE CAR PARK AT THE PUB, WITH PERMISSION.

The attractive village of Speldhurst is set in the lovely wooded countryside of the High Weald. It is an ancient parish, with a recorded history dating back to the 13th century, and this is reflected in some of the old houses in the village. Although the church is not very old, having been rebuilt in 1871, it has some wonderful stained glass windows by Pre-Raphaelite artist Burne-Jones. The walk goes through woodland that is particularly delightful in spring and autumn.

The George & Dragon

The half-timbered George & Dragon is probably one of the oldest inns in Britain, having been built in the early 13th century. Kentish bowmen are reputed to have celebrated here on their return from the battle of Agincourt, and there may be underground passages to the church. Inside the inn, you can sense this long history as the comfortable bars have beams, large flagstones and huge inglenook fireplaces. It remains a good place to celebrate, with a separate dining area and a fine choice of food and drink. The ales are from Harveys, Bass and the local Larkins brewery, and an extensive range of wines and whiskies is on offer. As for food, starters include giant field mushrooms with Welsh rarebit, while steaks, own recipe sausages and mash, and steak, ale and mushroom pie are among the main dishes. There are also daily specials such as moules marinière and grilled cod provençal, as well as a vegetarian choice, and sandwiches and trencherman's platters are available. The little garden at the front of the pub has a pleasant outlook across to the church. The pub is open all day Monday to Saturday, 11 am to 11 pm and on Sunday from 12 noon to 10.30 pm.

Food is served from 12 noon to 2.30 pm on Monday and Tuesday, 12 noon to 2.30 pm and 7 pm to 9 pm on Wednesday and Thursday, 12 noon to 3 pm and 7 pm to 10 pm on Friday and Saturday and 12 noon to 5 pm on Sunday. Telephone: 01892 863125.

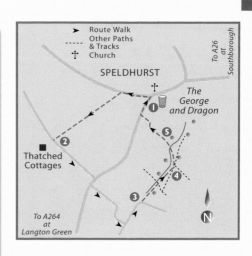

The Walk

NB: Be prepared for some muddy sections in the woodland after rain.

① Carefully cross the road in front of the pub to the path opposite and turn left past the lychgate of the church, then continue straight on along Penshurst Road. Take a footpath on the left after 200 yards at a metal gate opposite September Cottage; this path forms part of two long-distance walks, the Wealdway and the Tunbridge Wells Circular. Keep straight on between gardens, then fields, as a fine view appears on the right. The path then goes between overhanging hedges and downhill to a minor road.

② Turn left on the road, but first it is worth a short diversion to the right to view a fine group of 15th century cottages. Follow the road left for $^1/_2$ mile to a junction and cross over with care to another minor road a short distance to the right. Walk along this road for another $^1/_3$ mile to a T-junction with another lane and turn left.

Speldhurst church

③ After about 400 yards, where this lane bends right, go straight on over a stile hidden in the hedge and down the field to another stile at the far end. Keep straight ahead, to the right of trees, to shortly enter a wood at a stile. Where the path widens out after 100 yards go straight on between wooden posts. The path continues through the wood for some time, going over a pathway of wooden poles in the wettest parts, and with a stream on the left. Where it joins another track near a wooden marker post turn left.

④ Go past a footpath coming in from the right, then where the path forks take the left fork with a Tunbridge Wells Circular marker. The path continues through woodland, crosses a stream by a bridge, then goes gradually uphill to a stile to leave the wood.

⑤ Continue between hedges to the drive to a house. Turn left along this long drive to a road, then go right to return to Speldhurst church and the pub.

PLACES OF INTEREST NEARBY

The **Spa Valley Railway** runs steam trains from Tunbridge Wells to Groombridge. Open at weekends from April to October and on some weekdays from July to September. Telephone: 01892 537715. **Groombridge Place**, off the B2110 south of Langton Green, has walled gardens, woodland walks and an adventure trail. Open daily from April to October. Telephone: 01892 863999.

Shipbourne
The Chaser

MAP: OS EXPLORER 147 (GR 592522) | **WALK 7** | **DISTANCE:** 3½ MILES

DIRECTIONS TO START: SHIPBOURNE IS 4 MILES NORTH OF TONBRIDGE ON THE A227, WITH THE PUB TO THE WEST OF THE MAIN ROAD, OPPOSITE THE COMMON. **PARKING:** IN THE PUB CAR PARK, WITH PERMISSION, OR ALONGSIDE THE COMMON. THE WALK COULD ALSO BE JOINED FROM THE CAR PARK AT IGHTHAM MOTE, POINT 4, OPEN DAILY.

This walk goes through delightful countryside on the edge of the Greensand Ridge, where the woods are glorious in autumn as the leaves change colour and in spring as bluebells and other woodland flowers bloom. There are far-reaching views over the Weald and, as a bonus, you pass one of the loveliest moated houses in Britain, Ightham Mote, which dates from the 14th century.

The Chaser

This inn was built in the colonial style in the 1880s and occupies a pleasant position overlooking the large common at Shipbourne (pronounced Shibbon). It has two bars, decorated with paintings featuring horses, relevant because the nearby mansion at Fairlawne was, until recently, owned by the famous horse racing family of Cazelet. There is also a separate restaurant with a beamed, vaulted ceiling.

The menu here is extensive and imaginative, examples being chicken breast stuffed with mandarin in a brie and bacon sauce, sea bass and scallops. There are also daily specials such as duck with black cherry sauce and cheese and asparagus quiche with salad. Bar meals include steaks, gammon, scampi and an enormous mixed grill, while sandwiches, ploughman's lunches and jacket potatoes are available too. Drinks on offer include Harveys and Morland Old Speckled Hen ales, Beamish Black stout, Foster's lager and Strongbow cider. The pub is open all day Monday to Saturday from 11 am to 11 pm and from 12 noon to 10.30 pm on Sunday.

Food is served from 12 noon to 2.30 pm and 6.30 pm to 9.30 pm Monday to Saturday and 12 noon to 4 pm and 6.30 pm to 8.30 pm on Sunday. Telephone: 01732 810360.

The Walk

NB. There may be some muddy sections after rain.

① Go through the lychgate of the adjacent church and follow the path

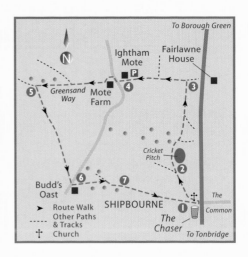

through the churchyard, then go immediately right over a stile. Head diagonally left across a field to two stiles in quick succession and continue past trees on the right to another stile.

② Turn right along a stony track to skirt a cricket field. Just past the pavilion cross another track to continue on a grassy track with a hedge on the left, then through a pedestrian gate and along the left edge of a field.

③ About 100 yards before an avenue of trees ahead, turn left through a wooden gate next to a telegraph pole. Fairlawne mansion is level with you, glimpsed through trees on the right. The footpath goes between low hedges and eventually joins a road by the car park at Ightham Mote (tearoom open to non-visitors). Continue past the lovely house to a road by gates.

④ Turn right for 50 yards, then left on a farm road, which swings right past an oasthouse then becomes a stony track.

The south front of Ightham Mote

Once a route between Ightham Mote and Knole House at Sevenoaks, this is now part of the Greensand Way (GSW). Keep on the track, following GSW signs, for ¾ mile, until you reach an isolated house on the right.

⑤ Go left here at a stile, signposted 'Little Budds', with fantastic views over the Weald. Go down the field to another stile, then along the right edge of two fields, over a plank bridge and between fields to a minor road.

⑥ Turn right for 15 yards, then over a stile on the left, just before Budd's Oast. The path climbs gradually between trees. Keep straight on, ignoring any side paths, until

you come to a complex junction of paths. Here go slightly right for a few yards, then take the left fork. A field can be seen on the left through a strip of trees.

⑦ Leaving the wood at a stile, go straight ahead across a large field towards the church, and continue to the right of a hedge to return to the churchyard and the inn.

> **PLACES OF INTEREST NEARBY**
> **Ightham Mote** (National Trust) is one of the finest moated manor houses in the country, over 650 years old, and has gardens and woodland walks. Open from April to October (not Tuesday and Saturday). Telephone: 01732 811145.

West Peckham
The Swan

MAP: OS EXPLORER 148 (GR 644525)   **WALK 8**   **DISTANCE:** 2¾ MILES

DIRECTIONS TO START: TURN NORTH OFF THE A26 AT ITS JUNCTION WITH THE A228 NEAR MEREWORTH, ONTO THE B2016. TAKE THE FIRST LEFT, AND AFTER ¾ MILE KEEP STRAIGHT ON TO THE VILLAGE GREEN, WITH THE PUB TO THE LEFT.
PARKING: IN THE PUB CAR PARK, WITH PERMISSION.

The small village of West Peckham occupies a lovely position at the base of heavily wooded hills. It is prime fruit growing country, and there are orchards all around, as well as plantations of raspberries, strawberries and blackcurrants. Several very old buildings add to the charm of the area. The village centre forms a quintessentially English scene, with an ancient church and pub on the edge of the green and cricket pitch. What finer sight can there be on a summer's day, with a match in progress?

The Swan

This delightful inn has formed part of the village's idyllic rural centre for a very long time, the building dating from 1526, though later alterations have been made. It was licensed in 1685, but has also been a bakery for part of its history. It has its own microbrewery, producing cask-conditioned ales such as Trumpeter and Whooper Pale, and also Black Swan stout and green hop and organic beers. There is also a good choice of food, for example home-smoked salmon salad, Barbary duck breast with orange and whisky sauce, red bream fillet cooked in sweet paprika and such novel selections as ribeye steak marinated in beer and nettles topped with a hop cheese. The meals are served in comfortable bars with a log fire in winter and beams decorated with dried hops . You can also sit outside on the edge of the green – just watch out for flying cricket balls in summer!

The pub is open from 11 am to 3 pm and 6 pm to 11 pm on weekdays, 11 am to 4 pm and 6 pm to 11 pm on Saturday and 12 noon to 4 pm and 7 pm to 9 pm on Sunday, and food is served from 12 noon to 2 pm and 7.30 pm to 9.30 pm. Telephone: 01622 812271.

The Walk

① Go right from the pub towards the church and follow the track around the right side of the cricket field to a metal kissing gate. Continue straight on along a farm track and straight across a farm road by Pear Tree Cottage to a stile in the hedge 10 yards on the right, then keep to the right edge of a field.

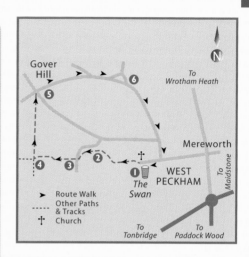

② Where the windbreak of poplars on the right ends go left to follow the field edge around (not over the stile ahead). Continue between tall hedges, then turn left on a road for 50 yards past a stone cottage.

③ Go right at a footpath sign for the Wealdway and Greensand Way paths along a wide track. The stony track goes gradually uphill, with fine views to the left. On reaching trees on the right go through a gap at a marker post and along the left edge of a field with cane fruit, then apples. Near the top of the field go over a stile hidden in the hedge on the left and continue for 30 yards to a crossroads of paths.

④ Turn right here along a path between wire fences (part of the Wealdway), with orchards on both sides. The track climbs gradually, with superb views back and to the left, and comes out at a complex road junction at Gover Hill.

⑤ Take the narrow Peckham Hurst Road at second right (1 o'clock) as it goes uphill between trees. The woods on the left are

On the walk

mostly of sweet chestnut, which is cut periodically to make fence posts and hop poles. At a T-junction after almost ½ mile turn right and ¼ mile later, just past a private drive on the right, keep right where the road forks and follow it between tall hazel hedges to another T-junction.

⑥ Turn right here and soon enjoy a wonderful view over the Medway valley and the Weald as the road drops steeply down. At a road junction keep straight on down Forge Lane, then at the next T-junction turn right to return to the church and the pub.

PLACES OF INTEREST NEARBY

Great Comp Garden, 4 miles north, off the B2016, is a 7 acre garden with a wide variety of plants. Open daily from April to October. Telephone: 01732 886154. At Hadlow, south of West Peckham on the A26 you will find **Broadview Gardens** – 16 acres of themed and landscaped gardens, plus a plant centre. Open daily from March to October. Telephone: 01732 850551.

Trottiscliffe
The George

| MAP: OS EXPLORER 148 (GR 641599) | WALK 9 | DISTANCE: 3 MILES |

DIRECTIONS TO START: TROTTISCLIFFE CAN BE REACHED ON MINOR ROADS FROM THE A20 BETWEEN WROTHAM AND MAIDSTONE OR THE A227 BETWEEN WROTHAM AND GRAVESEND. **PARKING:** THE PUB HAS A LARGE CAR PARK FOR PATRONS. PLEASE ASK PERMISSION TO LEAVE THE CAR THERE WHILE WALKING.

Trottiscliffe is an attractive village which lies at the foot of the south-facing slope of the North Downs. The first surprise is that it is pronounced 'Trosley' by the locals. There are lovely weatherboarded cottages and conversions of typical Kent oasthouses. We step back in time to follow old trackways and pass close to an ancient burial ground, known as the Coldrum Stones. This site is the remains of a Neolithic long barrow, built in the third millennium BC. The bones of a family of 22 people were excavated from the tomb chamber in 1912. Most of the huge standing stones have fallen, but there is still a wonderful atmosphere of peace and history here. We return to the village past the picturesque Norman church. The walk has wonderful views across the lovely countryside of mid-Kent and in spring and summer lots of colourful wild flowers and butterflies can be seen.

The George

This homely village pub was built in 1636 as a dwelling house and it was first registered as a licensed inn in 1812. The timbered bars have cosy alcoves and an inglenook fireplace, and dried hops are draped over the beams. There is a wide range of food, which can be eaten in the bar area or in the separate dining room. The menu includes various savoury puddings such as chicken and leek, as well as steak dishes, racks of lamb or ribs, salmon pasta florentine and vegetable and leek crumble. There is also a selection of tempting desserts. Rolls, sandwiches and ploughman's lunches are available too. Beers include Wadworth 6X, Boddingtons and Shepherd Neame Master Brew. There is a small but well-chosen wine list, including three champagnes. Outdoors there are tables at the front of the pub and in the garden. Families are welcome.

Opening hours are 11.30 am to 3 pm and 6 pm to 11 pm on Monday to Saturday and all day on Sunday. Food is served from 12 noon to 2.30 pm and from 6 pm to 11 pm Monday to Saturday and on Sunday from 12 noon to 2.30 pm and 7 pm to 11 pm. Telephone: 01732 822462.

The Walk

① From the car park turn left up the main street, ignoring a road on the right. At a crossroads go straight on past a duckpond on the left.

② About 50 yards on, turn right up Green Lane and where the metalled lane ends go straight on at the 'Public Bridleway' sign.

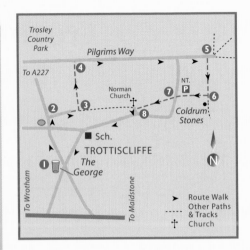

③ At the end of the wooden fence on the left turn left past the ends of gardens, then go on across a field. Continue with a hedge on the left until you reach the base of the Downs. It is worth a look back at the lovely views.

④ You reach a kissing gate next to a metal gate. Opposite this is one of the entrances to Trosley Country Park, but the walk turns right on the metalled road. You are now on the Pilgrims' Way, following in the footsteps of the medieval pilgrims who trekked to Canterbury. Continue along this road for almost a mile, with the overhanging trees forming a cool green tunnel on a hot day.

⑤ Where the road ends at a white-brick house on the left, take a footpath off to the right at a wooden post with yellow arrows and a WW (Wealdway) sign. The path goes down, away from the hills, and can be slippery in places after wet weather. There are fine views ahead, and to the Medway valley in the left distance. After passing between two wooden posts, you come to another post which has yellow arrows.

Trottiscliffe's Norman church

⑥ Turn right here. However, it is worth taking a short diversion first to see the Coldrum Stones. To do so go straight on for 100 yards and look for the National Trust sign on the right. After visiting the Stones retrace your steps to point 6 and turn left.

The path goes across a field, then continues with a hedge on the left and later between fences, then hedges. There is a short stretch of metalled track before a road is reached.

⑦ Go straight across to a wooden post and cross the field ahead. Soon a lovely view appears of Trottiscliffe church, nestling among trees. The path continues to a road by the church.

⑧ Pause to admire the church and adjacent picturesque cottages, then turn left on the road. After 50 yards turn right at the T-junction. Follow this road, and where it forks by the village school take the left fork, which ends opposite the George.

> **PLACES OF INTEREST NEARBY**
> **Trosley Country Park**, which occupies 160 acres of grassland and woodland on the North Downs, is owned by Kent County Council and has a visitor centre, reached by a road from the A227. Telephone: 01732 823570.

Cobham
The Old Leather Bottle

DIRECTIONS TO START: COBHAM IS 1 MILE SOUTH OF THE A2(T) BETWEEN GRAVESEND AND STROOD, NEAR THE WESTERN END OF THE M2. THE PUB IS IN THE MAIN STREET, OPPOSITE THE CHURCH. **PARKING:** IN THE PUB CAR PARK, WITH PERMISSION, OR IN THE PUBLIC CAR PARK FURTHER EAST ALONG THE MAIN STREET, BEHIND THE SCHOOL.

The picturesque village of Cobham is situated on the North Downs and has strong associations with Charles Dickens, who lived nearby and often walked in the area. The village also has a lovely 13th century church, which has a wonderful set of medieval brasses, possibly the best in the country. There is also an interesting 14th century building, which was a college for priests. Nearby is a grandiose Elizabethan mansion, Cobham Hall.

This walk provides glimpses into the rich history of the area, as well as taking you through some of the delightful landscapes of the rolling chalk hills to the south of the village. You can choose to return from point 5, but the slightly longer circuit gives you the opportunity to pass an ancient wood, plus the parkland of Cobham Hall.

The Old Leather Bottle

This lovely half-timbered inn, built in 1629, got its name when a leather bottle containing gold sovereigns was found in 1720. Charles Dickens was a frequent visitor and used the inn as a model for the one in *Pickwick Papers*. The inn is full of Dickens memorabilia, including paintings and etchings. A good choice of food is available in the timbered bars, with roasts, steaks, pies, curries and daily specials. There are also omelettes, salads, sandwiches, jacket potatoes, ploughman's lunches and baguettes with hot or cold fillings. These can be followed by delicious desserts such as banana, toffee and rum pudding, plum pudding or chocolate fudge cake. Courage Best, Shepherd Neame Spitfire and John Smith's bitters are on offer.

The pub is open from 11 am to 11 pm, with food served from 12.30 pm to 2.30 pm and 7 pm to 9.30 pm. Telephone: 01474 814327.

The Walk

① Cross the road in front of the inn and go up steps into the churchyard. Take the path to the right of the church entrance and then left of a wooden seat. Continue under overhanging trees, past the ancient college on the left, then left of a graveyard and over a stile.

② Continue downhill along the right edge of a field, with lovely views, and at the end of the field go through a gap in trees to a lane.

③ Turn left over a railway, then soon go right on a footpath just before Batts

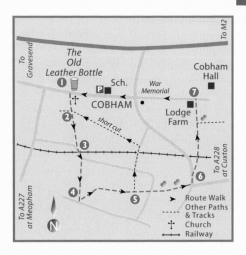

Cottages. Keep to the left edge of the field, then go through a hedge and scrub to a kissing gate. Cross a small field to another gate, then continue down through the field ahead.

④ At the bottom of the field turn back diagonally uphill on the path to the left, to a gap in the hedge at the top, and continue along the top of the next field, with views ahead.

⑤ After 500 yards there is a post with two arrows. *For the shorter route*, turn left up the bank and take the path up through the field. On reaching a minor road at a junction take the road straight ahead. After 600 yards take a footpath on the left and go diagonally across the field to return to point 2, where you turn right and continue through the churchyard to reach the Old Leather Bottle again.

For the longer walk, go straight on at the post to a road. Turn left for 20 yards then right at a wooden post. Continue for 400 yards with a wood on the left, colourful with bluebells in spring. The path turns left

Elizabethan Cobham Hall

under telephone wires, but after 20 yards turn right, away from the wires, on a path through the wood.

⑥ On emerging from the wood turn sharp left up a road for 150 yards, then take a metalled track on the right, to go under a railway and later to the left of a wood.

⑦ On reaching a T-junction with a wider track turn left until you reach a road on a bend next to a war memorial. Cross the

road and go straight ahead along Cobham's main street to return to the car park and the inn.

PLACES OF INTEREST NEARBY

Cobham Hall is a large mansion dating from 1584, with lovely interiors. It is now a school, but is open on certain dates, with guided tours. Telephone: 01474 823371.

Matfield
The Standing's Cross

| MAP: OS EXPLORER 136 (GR 661421) | WALK 11 | DISTANCE: 3 MILES |

DIRECTIONS TO START: MATFIELD IS EAST OF TUNBRIDGE WELLS, 2 MILES NORTH OF THE A21 ON THE B2160, WITH THE PUB AT THE NORTH END OF THE VILLAGE.
PARKING: IN THE PUB CAR PARK, WITH PERMISSION.

The centre of Matfield is quintessentially English, with a charming village green that includes a cricket field and a duckpond. Lovely buildings are grouped around the green, among them Matfield House, an impressive Queen Anne style house with clocktower built in the early 18th century, and a fine row of 17th century cottages.

The countryside around Matfield is also delightful. The area has long been a centre of the fruit growing industry and you will see orchards of apples and pears on this stroll, as well as plantations of cobnuts, a type of hazelnut. In spring the orchards provide a fantastic display of white and pink blossom. The gently rolling landscape is also well wooded, offering glorious backdrops as you walk.

The Standing's Cross

This inn was founded by John Standing in about 1850, in what had been a bakery. He had previously run an alehouse from the cottages opposite, but needed larger premises. The pub now serves fine food in the comfortable roomy bars. As well as the extensive main menu, several specials of the day are offered. When I visited these included tenderloin of pork with an apple and Calvados sauce and Barbary duck breast with a port and redcurrant sauce. In addition there are steak and fish dishes, pies, ploughman's lunches, sandwiches and baked potatoes, as well as vegetarian and children's meals. Children are also catered for with a small adventure playground in the garden. There is a good selection of ales, including Courage Directors, Marston's Pedigree, Wadworth 6X, John Smith's and several lagers.

Opening hours are 12 noon to 3 pm and 5 pm to 11 pm on Sunday to Friday and all day on Saturday. Food is served from 12 noon to 2.30 pm and 6.30 pm to 9.30 pm every day. Telephone: 01892 722416.

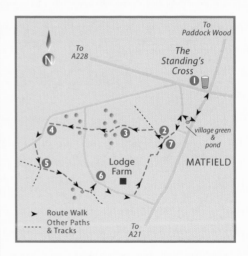

The Walk

① Turn right down the main village street to the duckpond, right round the green to the cricket pavilion, then right at a footpath signpost down a drive past Lees Court.

② Where a fence ends go right on a foot-path, then after 200 yards left over a stile and diagonally right across a field to a marker post near a telegraph post. Go left through bushes then diagonally sharp right across a field to a stile into a wood.

③ Follow the path as it winds through rather primeval-looking vegetation and from the wood go straight across a small field to a minor road and turn right. After 40 yards go left into another wood and uphill through trees, with bluebells in spring. Where the wood ends turn right to follow the right edge of orchards of cobnuts and apples. After 300 yards cross a stile near metal gates to reach a minor road.

④ Go left for 250 yards, then left down a drive between houses, going to the right of the last white-boarded house, and through a white gate. Continue straight ahead through an orchard to a stile hidden in the hedge.

⑤ Over the stile turn sharp left, keeping to the left edge of two fields, then go through a hedge and straight ahead through another cobnut plantation. Enter a wood near a post, then go downhill near the edge of the wood, before crossing a

Matfield village pond

stream. Go over a stile, past a pond, and straight up a field to a stile in a gap in trees. Turn left up a gravel track, then left where it joins another track, to a minor road.

⑥ Turn right for 250 yards then left at a stile. Keep to the right edge of two fields, with lovely views left. At a third field aim slightly right to a post in a gap in the hedge, then diagonally left across a field to a stile in a wooden fence. Keep left of a low fence then turn right around an oasthouse to its drive and left to return to point 2.

⑦ Go straight on to the village green, then left to return to the pub.

PLACES OF INTEREST NEARBY

The **Hop Farm Country Park** at Beltring, 4 miles north of Matfield, has shire horses, farm animals, a pets' corner, an adventure playground and exhibitions. Open daily. Telephone: 01622 872068.

Lamberhurst
The Chequers

MAP: OS EXPLORER 136 (GR 677363)   WALK 12   **DISTANCE:** 1¾ MILES

DIRECTIONS TO START: LAMBERHURST IS 6 MILES SOUTH-EAST OF TUNBRIDGE WELLS, ON THE A21. THE PUB AND ADJACENT PUBLIC CAR PARK ARE ON THE EAST SIDE OF THE MAIN STREET. **PARKING:** IN THE PUB CAR PARK, WITH PERMISSION, OR THE ADJACENT PUBLIC CAR PARK.

Lamberhurst is set in lovely rolling countryside and the village has some attractive houses. Though it is hard to imagine now, this area was once the centre of the iron industry, but today there are few signs, apart from some hammer ponds used to power the mills. There is an ancient church on a hill away from the main street, but passed on the walk, and nearby is the romantic ruin of Scotney Castle, now under the care of the National Trust. The walk is somewhat hilly, but you are rewarded with superb views.

The Chequers

This old coaching inn, now adapted to modern requirements, still has timber beams and an enormous inglenook fireplace. There are spacious bars and a welcome non-smoking area, as well as a garden. A good selection of food includes tuna steak, mussels and Peking style lemon chicken, also daily specials such as rib-eye steak with brandy and mushroom sauce and lamb with rosemary, thyme and cranberry jus. Among the lighter snacks are ploughman's lunches and tortilla wraps. A walk-induced appetite will find room for the inviting desserts, for example toffee apple and pecan crumble or treacle sponge. Several Shepherd Neame ales are available, including Spitfire and Goldings summer ale, in addition to Scrumpy Jack cider and an extensive wine list.

Opening times are 11 am to 11 pm, with food available from 12 noon to 2.30 pm and 7 pm to 9.30 pm on Monday to Saturday and 12 noon to 9 pm on Sunday. Telephone: 01892 890260

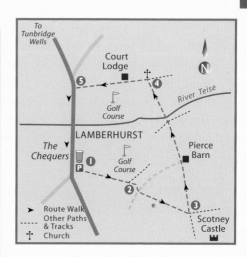

The Walk

① From the rear of the public car park go through a wooden gate and straight across a sports field, then across a second field with football pitches to its far right hand corner. Go through a gap in the hedge to a golf course. Keep to the hedge on the right, following a line of short yellow posts, then cross a golf fairway with caution to a stile. Continue straight ahead past a golf tee to a gap in a newly-planted hedge.

② Go straight across a small field to a concrete track and turn right along it for 60 yards before going left across a field to a post with yellow arrow in the hedge. Keep to the right hand edge of the next field as you go uphill with a wood on the right. There are glorious views across to Lamberhurst church on the left.

③ At the end of the field turn sharp left to go downhill along the edge of the field with a hedge on your right. (Note: if you go right at point 3 you enter the Scotney Castle Estate and you can walk to the entrance from there.) At the bottom of the field go straight across a concrete track and through a gap in the hedge. The path goes ahead past three trees then bears left, aiming for the church in the distance. Cross a bridge over the river then go straight up the field to the church.

④ On reaching a stile at the edge of the churchyard turn sharp left along its bottom edge. At the church noticeboard go through an open gateway to a tarmac path. It is worth pausing to take a look around

Looking towards Lamberhurst church

the ancient church and to admire the fine views from the churchyard. Follow the tarmac path along the edge of the golf course and past Court Lodge mansion on the right until you reach the main road.

⑤ Turn left to follow the road through the village back to the pub and car park.

PLACES OF INTEREST NEARBY

Scotney Castle Garden (National Trust) – a superb garden surrounding the remains of the moated 14th century castle. Open from April to October (closed Monday and Tuesday). Telephone: 01892 891081. **Bewl Water**, to the south of Lamberhurst, is the largest lake in the south-east and provides walks, boat trips, watersports and a visitor centre. Open daily. Telephone: 01892 890661.

Goudhurst
The Star and Eagle

DIRECTIONS TO START: GOUDHURST IS 4 MILES WEST OF CRANBROOK, ON THE A262. THE INN IS AT THE EAST END OF THE VILLAGE, WITH ITS CAR PARK REACHED BY A MINOR ROAD EAST OF THE CHURCH. FOR THE PUBLIC CAR PARK TURN SOUTH ON THE B2079 BY THE DUCKPOND. **PARKING:** IN THE PUB CAR PARK, WITH PERMISSION, OR IN THE PUBLIC CAR PARK (GR 723376).

Goudhurst is a very attractive village, with typical Kentish white weather-boarded houses, a large duckpond and an historic church with fine memorial tombs. The area became prosperous in the Middle Ages, when the woollen industry flourished. The village is perched on a hill and has lovely views of the surrounding countryside, which is typical of the High Weald, with scenic hills and valleys. Traditionally this has been fruit and hop growing country, and although these types of farming have suffered a decline in recent years, you will still see orchards and hop gardens on the walk.

The Star and Eagle

The long history of this pub can be traced back to the 14th century, and at one time it was the headquarters of a notorious gang of smugglers. It has a fine exterior, with timbers and a balcony, and inside there are spacious bars and a separate eating area, with beams and an inglenook fireplace adding to the historical atmosphere. There are seats on the patio at the rear too, with fabulous views over the Wealden countryside.

The fine food on offer includes the speciality moules et frites, mushroom crêpes, roast shoulder of lamb Spanish style, monkfish tails, chicken fajitas and steak, mushroom and ale pie, also daily specials. Among the enticing desserts are chocolate truffle torte, pannecotta and profiteroles. Several beers are available, including Adnams and Boddingtons, and there is an extensive wine list.

Opening times are 11 am to 11 pm on Monday to Saturday and 12 noon to 10.30 pm on Sunday, with food served from 12 noon to 2.30 pm and 7 pm to 9 pm. Telephone: 01580 211512/211338.

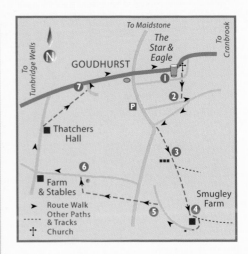

The Walk

① Turn right from the front of the inn into the churchyard and by the church entrance turn right down a path with handrail to a road. Cross to the footpath opposite and go downhill between fields, then down steps to another minor road. (From the public car park cross the road and go down the lane ahead for 250 yards to join the walk at point 2.)

② Turn left for 20 yards, then where the road forks take the right fork. Just before this road joins another go left down a track next to a house with a black and white wall. On reaching a metal gate on the right, go over a stile into a field. Keep to the left edge, skirting a riding paddock, and at the field's end cross a stile to a road in front of some new houses.

③ Go down a path next to the left end house and keep straight on, ignoring a path that goes off left. Continue between hedges, then meadows, with views back to the church on the hill.

④ On reaching buildings and a wooden fence go left between concrete posts, then right at a marker post with a wooden fence on the right. At the next marker post ignore the left-pointing arrow to go straight on, then follow a road past a converted oasthouse, once used for drying hops, then round a bend.

⑤ Cross a stream, then as the road bends right go off left at a marker post to follow

The delightful countryside around Goudhurst

the route of an old railway line, reaching a road at the third stile. Cross with care and go down steps opposite. Keep to the left edge across two fields, then after a metal pedestrian gate about 200 yards before stables turn sharp right along a field edge, then left of a small wood to reach a minor road.

⑥ Turn left to a T-junction then right up Ranters Lane for 400 yards to a footpath on the right, next to the drive of Thatchers Hall. Keep to the right edge of two fields, to a narrow path between gardens.

⑦ At its end go straight ahead to the main A262 and turn right alongside it to return to the village, with fine views to the left.

PLACES OF INTEREST NEARBY
Bedgebury Pinetum, off the B2079 to the south, has over 2,000 types of tree and is beautifully landscaped around lakes, with a visitor centre and tearooms. Open daily. Telephone: 01580 211044. **Finchcocks**, off the A262 just west of Goudhurst, is an 18th century manor with a fine collection of historical keyboard instruments. Open on Sundays and Bank Holiday Mondays from Easter to September, plus Wednesdays and Thursdays in August. Telephone: 01580 211702.

Yalding
The Walnut Tree

MAP: OS EXPLORERS 148 AND 136 (GR 699503)   **WALK 14**   **DISTANCE:** 1¾ MILES

DIRECTIONS TO START: YALDING IS 6 MILES SW OF MAIDSTONE, ON THE B2010. APPROACHING FROM THE NORTH, THE PUB IS ON THE RIGHT, SHORTLY AFTER ENTERING THE VILLAGE. **PARKING:** IN THE PUB CAR PARK, WITH PERMISSION.

The village of Yalding is in a prime position at the confluence of three major rivers – the Medway, Teise and Beult. Of these, the Beult runs through the centre of the village, and is crossed by a narrow medieval stone bridge. The ancient church, with its unusual onion-shaped dome, stands next to the river, and there are lovely cottages and large Georgian houses lining the main street. This is the heart of the hop and fruit growing area of mid-Kent and the walk takes you past some old orchards and provides an opportunity to see some of the interesting buildings in this delightful village.

The Walnut Tree

This 15th century building has a lovely bar and a separate restaurant area, both with beams and large inglenook fireplaces. As befits its location, the Walnut Tree is decorated not only with hops, but also hop memorabilia such as hop sacks and interesting photographs of past eras when the hops were picked by hand.

There is a good choice of food and drink, served in a friendly manner. The main menu includes fillet steak in a burgundy, port, mushroom and shallot sauce, rack of lamb, salmon tagliatelle, stir fried vegetables with Chinese noodles, and mushroom stroganoff. Among the bar meals are steak, Guinness and mushroom pie, lamb and tomato casserole and corned beef and potato hash. There are also several fresh fish selections, for example bream with a ginger and spring onion sauce, plaice and sardines. Some of the desserts use local fruit, so you might find apple pancakes or hot black cherries with a hint of brandy. Lighter snacks include baguettes, salads and ploughman's lunches. Several beers are available, including Adnams, King and Barnes, Greene King IPA and Tetley's, plus a guest ale each month such as Everards Equinox. Also on offer are Guinness, Strongbow cider, Heineken and Stella Artois lagers , wines and local apple and pear juices.

Opening times are 11.45 am to 3 pm and 6 pm to 11 pm Monday to Saturday and 12 noon to 10.30 pm on Sunday, with food served from 12 noon to 2.30 pm and 6.30 pm to 9.30 pm. Telephone: 01622 814266.

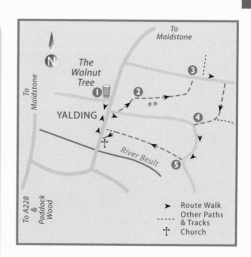

The Walk

① Cross the road in front of the pub to the war memorial and go up Vicarage Road ahead. After 40 yards go left on a footpath, part of the Greensand Way. Go past a wall plaque with a poem by Siegfried Sassoon, and past almshouses on the right to a road in a small housing estate. Go left for 80 yards, then right up Mount Avenue.

② Where this road ends continue straight on along a footpath through trees, and later with a hedge on the right. The path swings left, with on the right a traditional apple orchard with tall old trees and often sheep grazing beneath, a rare sight nowadays.

③ On reaching a minor road turn right along it, between tall hedges. After ¼ mile, just before the first house on the right, go right at a footpath sign by a wooden fence. Continue with a stream on the right, later obscured by trees. Keep to the left of these trees until you reach a farm road and turn right.

Yalding village

④ When you reach a T-junction with another road you can turn right to return to the village but for the full walk turn left. Follow the road with care through bends for 400 yards and look for a footpath sign on the right by a wooden kissing gate.

⑤ Go through the gate to a path that is first wide and grassy, then becomes narrower with a hedge on the right. Continue along the right edge of a sports field and to the right of a playground. Keep straight on until the churchyard is reached on the left. To view the church and medieval bridge go diagonally left through the churchyard and down to the road, where you turn left to the bridge and right to return to the pub.

> **PLACES OF INTEREST NEARBY**
> **Yalding Organic Gardens** are just to the south of the village. There are 14 gardens in styles from medieval to present day, all grown organically, also a gift shop, an organic café and plants for sale. Open Wednesday to Sunday from May to September and at weekends in April and October. Telephone: 01622 814650.

Linton
The Bull

MAP: OS EXPLORERS 148 AND 136 (GR 754502) — **WALK 15** — **DISTANCE:** 2, 2¾ OR 3¼ MILES

DIRECTIONS TO START: LYING ON THE A229, LINTON IS 4 MILES SOUTH OF MAIDSTONE, FROM WHICH DIRECTION THE PUBLIC CAR PARK IS ON THE LEFT, AND THE PUB SHORTLY AFTERWARDS ON THE RIGHT. **PARKING:** IN THE LARGE PUBLIC CAR PARK, OR THE PUB CAR PARK, WITH PERMISSION.

This walk goes along the Greensand Ridge, with wonderful long-distance views over the Kentish Weald. It also shows why Kent is known as the garden of England, as it passes through orchards of apples and pears, which provide a glorious display of fragrant blossom in early May. There are also fine parkland trees to see, the handsome white mansion of Linton Place, 'the citadel of Kent', and ancient churches, making this a walk of varied interest. Two shortcuts are possible (see map). Be prepared for some gradual climbs.

The Bull

This 17th century coaching inn lies on the main route between Maidstone and the south coast. Its long history is still evident in the interior, with its beams and huge fireplace. The spacious bar and separate eating area both have imaginative choices of food. The bar menu includes sausages and mash with red wine sauce and a delicious fisherman's pie, while sandwiches are also available. Among the restaurant choices are steak, confit of duck leg, monkfish wrapped in Bayonne ham with mussels and saffron, and for vegetarians stuffed roasted pepper, red onion and Stilton tart. There are also tempting desserts such as lemon cheesecake with passion fruit sorbet and dark chocolate parfait with white chocolate sorbet and fresh raspberries. Shepherd Neame ales are on offer, for example Master Brew, Spitfire and Late Red Autumn Hop Ale, plus Oranjeboom and Holstein Export lagers, Strongbow cider, Guinness and a range of wines. From the garden at the rear you can enjoy a wonderful view over the countryside of the Weald to far-distant hills.

Opening times are 11 am to 3 pm and 6 pm to 11 pm, with food served from 12 noon to 2 pm and 7 pm to 9.30 pm. Telephone: 01622 743612.

The Walk

① Cross the main road in front of the inn with care to the church opposite. Go through the churchyard to a path between fences, part of the Greensand Way walk. Keep straight on this path for ½ mile, crossing the drive of Linton Place.

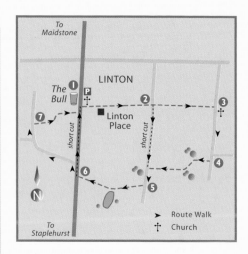

② On reaching a minor road go straight across to a gravel track. (*For a shorter route*, turn right down road for ½ mile to reach point 5.) Continue between hedges, then orchards, later with an alder windbreak on the left and fine views on the right, and through a gate to a minor road.

③ Turn right past Boughton Monchelsea church, worth a diversion, with its very old lychgate and tremendous views from the churchyard. Continue down the road and 100 yards past a lane on the left, go right over a stile at the end of a hedge.

④ Keep to the right edge of a field to a stile in the corner. Continue through a wood, where the path, marked by yellow-painted stakes, goes straight for a while then bends left near a metal gate. Emerge from the wood to a path between hedges, laden with berries and hips in autumn, then go over a stile and straight through an orchard to a minor road, where you turn left.

Orchard country

⑤ Just past a wood take a footpath at the end of a wire fence on the right, to go through scrub then along the right edge of a long field to a stile at the right corner of a wood, with views of Linton Place to the right. Go past a lake in trees on the left then diagonally right across the field to a stile onto the main road.

⑥ Cross the road and turn right on the path. *For a shortcut* you could continue up the hill back to the pub. Otherwise, turn left into Wheelers Lane and follow it for ½ mile, then go straight on up Vanity Lane to a stile on the right after 400 yards.

⑦ Follow a farm track and soon after it bends left go right at a stile and along the right edge of a field, towards the church ahead. Go up between hedges, then gardens, to the main road and turn left to the pub and the public car park beyond.

> **PLACES OF INTEREST NEARBY**
> **Iden Croft Herbs** at Staplehurst, a few miles south on the A229, has a walled garden with plant sales. Open from April to September. Telephone: 01580 891432. **Stoneacre** (National Trust) at Otham, reached from the A274 south-east of Maidstone, is a 15th century half-timbered house. Open from April to October on Wednesdays and Saturdays. Telephone: 01622 862871.

Aylesford
The Chequers

MAP: OS EXPLORER 148 (CAR PARK GR 732588)　　**WALK 16**　　**DISTANCE:** 2¼ MILES

DIRECTIONS TO START: AYLESFORD IS CLOSE TO JUNCTIONS 5 AND 6 OF THE M20. FROM JUNCTION 5 GO WEST ON THE A20 AND FOLLOW SIGNS FROM BRITISH LEGION VILLAGE. AYLESFORD PUBLIC CAR PARK IS ON THE LEFT AFTER 1 MILE, IMMEDIATELY AFTER CROSSING THE RIVER. **PARKING:** IN THE PUBLIC CAR PARK IN THE VILLAGE.

The Aylesford area has played a prominent part in English history, mainly because of its important position as the first easily fordable crossing of the river Medway from its estuary. Because of this it has been the scene of several battles, including one in the 5th century when the Jutes defeated the native British and went on to colonise Kent. The walk follows in the footsteps of these soldiers, and of pilgrims visiting the nearby Carmelite Friary, built in 1242. It crosses the 14th century ragstone bridge, passes the ancient church and other historic buildings in the village, and provides views of the North Downs, where Neolithic man built burial mounds.

The Chequers

This impressive black and white building, with bow-fronting and overhanging gables, dates from the 16th century. The historic feel continues inside, with low beams and large fireplaces in the roomy bars. Shot from flintlock pistols, found in these walls, were probably fired during an English Civil War battle in 1648. There are old photographs of the village decorating the walls. At the rear of the inn is a patio seating area overlooking the river.

There is a friendly welcome and a good choice of beers, with Morland Old Speckled Hen, Greene King IPA, Fuller's London Pride and Flowers, plus several lagers, Guinness and Strongbow cider. The pub is open every day from 12 noon to 11 pm (until 10.30 pm on Sunday). The lunchtime menu on Monday to Saturday features baguettes with hot fillings such as bacon, Brie and mushroom, doorstep sandwiches, burgers, jacket potatoes, ploughman's lunches and daily specials such as pork stir fry and moussaka. From 6 to 9 pm in the evenings and Sunday lunchtime noon to 3 pm there is a wider choice of main meals, including lamb rosemary, steak cacciatore, venison in red wine and Mediterranean pasta bake, plus roast meats on Sundays. Telephone: 01622 717286.

The Walk

① From the entrance to the public car park turn right to cross the river and admire the view of the medieval bridge with the gabled roofs of the village beyond,

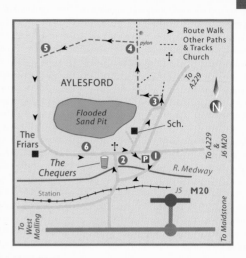

topped by the church. Continue to where the road bends left and turn right to cross the old bridge to the High Street.

② The Chequers is to the left here. To continue the walk go right for 80 yards then left up Mount Pleasant Road (not Church Walk). Follow this lane past a school and later a sand pit on the left.

③ Just past where a metalled track joins from the left go left at a footpath sign. The path runs beside a stream for a while, then continues along the left edge of a field, with views to the Downs on the right and left to Aylesford church over a huge sand quarry, which often has cormorants and gulls on its lake. Follow the field edge as it bends right and where the path forks go left through a belt of trees, with a wire fence on the left.

④ On reaching a narrow wood, just past power lines, turn left to walk parallel with the wires, to a road after 500 yards.

⑤ Turn left on the path alongside the road and follow it for ¾ mile back to the

Aylesford

village. There are sand pits on both sides of the road, but they are screened by trees and hedges of birch and field maple, festooned with old man's beard. Where the road bends left it is worth a diversion to view The Friars on the right, a restored 13th century priory with lovely buildings and cloisters and a tearoom in a medieval barn.

⑥ From the edge of the village you can either continue alongside the road to the Chequers or take the path through the churchyard. This has a view over the river to Preston Hall, a turreted mansion built in 1848. Where the church path ends, turn

right to return to the High Street. There is a pedestrian walkway going from the High Street opposite the bank and shop, then alongside the river back to the car park.

PLACES OF INTEREST NEARBY

The **Museum of Kent Life** at Sandling, near junction 6 of the M20, is an open air museum with historic buildings, exhibitions, gardens and farm animals. Open daily from March to October. Telephone: 01622 763936. **Tyland Barn**, just off the A229 east of Aylesford – Kent Wildlife Trust visitor centre with displays about local wildlife, a shop and a nature area. Open daily. Telephone: 01622 662012.

Thurnham
The Black Horse

MAP: OS EXPLORER 148 (GR 806579)   **WALK 17**   **DISTANCE:** 1½ OR 2½ MILES

DIRECTIONS TO START: LEAVING THE M20 AT JUNCTION 7, THURNHAM CAN BE REACHED ON MINOR ROADS FROM THE A249 AT DETLING OR THE A20 AT BEARSTED. THE PUB IS AT THE CROSSROADS IN THE HAMLET. **PARKING:** IN THE PUB CAR PARK, WITH PERMISSION, OR ALTERNATIVELY IN THE PUBLIC CAR PARK AT COBHAM MANOR RIDING CENTRE, FROM WHERE YOU WOULD START EITHER CIRCUIT AT POINT 3.

Thurnham occupies a fine position at the foot of the south-facing slope of the North Downs. It has a long history of settlement, with a Roman villa, an ancient church, a manor house and the site of a Norman castle in the parish. The longer walk has several steep ascents and descents, but, as compensation, there are wonderful views over the Kent countryside. There are also colourful chalkland flowers and butterflies to be seen in the summer months.

The Black Horse

The old Black Horse pub was devastated by fire in recent years, but the restoration has been so skilful that you would never know. There is a comfortable bar and an extensive dining area, where the beams, large fireplaces, wooden tables, and old casks and jugs give a sense of history. The menu is varied and imaginative, with starters such as smoked salmon with lime creme fraiche, main meals involving steak, lamb, venison, duck, sea bass and crab, and many tempting desserts. There are also lighter meals, a vegetarian selection, Sunday roasts, children's meals and sandwiches. Drinks include London Pride and Boddingtons beers, Heineken and Stella Artois lagers, Scrumpy Jack and Strongbow ciders, and an extensive wine list is available. For fine days there is a pleasant garden and a rear terrace with fine views.

Opening times are 11 am to 3 pm and 6 pm to 11 pm in the week and all day at weekends, with food served from 12 noon to 2.15 pm and 6.30 pm to 10 pm. Telephone: 01622 737185.

The Walk

① From the front of the pub go right for 10 yards to the crossroads. *For the longer walk*, turn left uphill on a minor road. After 300 yards, where the road bends to the left, take a footpath on the right, signposted 'North Downs Way'. Hidden in the dense vegetation on the left here are the remains of a castle. Follow the main, well-trodden path as it goes along the side of the Downs, soon with extensive views on the right.

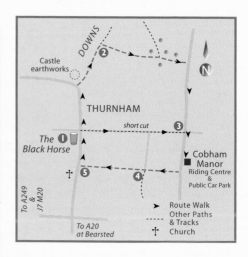

For the shorter, flatter walk, go straight ahead at the crossroads and continue along the road for ¾ mile to the turn for the riding centre at point 3.

② Go over a stile next to a metal gate and turn sharp right, keeping a wire fence on the right, to another stile. Look back for a good view of the earthworks of the castle. Go up wooden steps, then after a flat section, down more steps cut into the hillside. Climb more steps to a T-junction with another path and turn right. Follow this path to a minor road and turn right to descend from the Downs.

③ At a crossroads go straight across, to soon reach Cobham Manor Riding Centre on the left, where there are toilets and a café. Continue for 50 yards past the entrance to the centre and go over a stile in the hedge on the right. Go straight ahead along the right edge of a field, then over a stile to a minor road.

④ Keep straight on for 30 yards to where the road ends, then go through a wooden

The site of Thurnham's Norman castle

gate. Continue on a metalled road past a converted oasthouse on the left and follow it to a T-junction.

⑤ Turn right on the road to return to the pub, or take a short diversion to the left to see the ancient church and manor house.

PLACES OF INTEREST NEARBY

Leeds Castle is south-east of Thurnham and reached from the A20. It is one of the loveliest castles in Britain, and is surrounded by a moat and wonderful gardens, with an aviary, a maze, a restaurant and shops. Open daily. Telephone: 01622 765400.

Upnor
The King's Arms

DIRECTIONS TO START: UPNOR IS JUST NORTH OF ROCHESTER, NEAR THE JUNCTION OF THE A228 AND A289. THE PUB IS IN UPPER UPNOR, AT THE TOP OF THE STREET THAT LEADS DOWN TO THE RIVER AND CASTLE. **PARKING:** IN THE PUBLIC CAR PARK IN UPPER UPNOR OR, WITH PERMISSION, AT THE PUB.

The area in which this walk takes place is steeped in maritime history. The castle at Upnor, on the edge of the estuary of the river Medway, was built in the 16th century to guard the river from incursion by enemy fleets intent on attacking the naval dockyard at Chatham, further inland on the opposite side of the river. The river is now used for more pleasurable activities, with the sails of countless yachts creating lovely scenes, and interesting birdlife at low tide. Although the walk has a rather steep ascent and descent, you are rewarded with wonderful views along the estuary towards its merger with the Thames, and back to the cathedral and castle in Rochester. You can also see the restored Chatham Naval Dockyard on the opposite bank.

The King's Arms

The King's Arms in Upper Upnor is a friendly pub, with bars, a separate eating area, and a garden at the rear. It is at the top of the narrow main street in the village, with a view down to the river framed by old cottages. The castle is at the bottom of this street. Specialities on the menu include medallions of beef with a brandy, cream and mushroom sauce and pork loin with apple and Calvados. As befits the proximity to water there are fish dishes such as deep sea crab and tiger prawn salad and BBQ sailfish with seaweed. The tempting desserts on offer include strawberry and champagne roulade. You can also get bar snacks such as pies, omelettes, jacket potatoes, hot or cold baguettes and sandwiches. There is a good choice of ales, with Brains, Brakspears and Flowers on offer when I visited, in addition to lagers and Scrumpy Jack cider.

The pub is open from 11 am to 11 pm, and food is served from 12 noon to 2.30 pm (12 to 3 on Sunday) and 6.30 pm to 9.30 pm (no food on Sunday and Monday evenings). Telephone: 01634 717490.

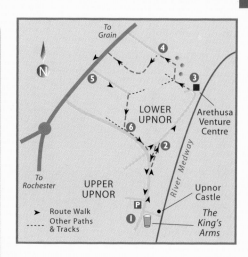

The Walk

① At the top of the street leading down to the river turn right facing away from the river and follow the path alongside a road. After 50 yards take the path alongside the right fork and continue beside the tall brick wall of Upnor Castle House and eventually down steps to a road.

② Turn right and follow the road into Lower Upnor, where there are other pubs. There are also lovely views along the river Medway and back to Upnor Castle. Walk along the concrete apron next to the river until you reach a stone obelisk.

(NB: The remainder of the walk has quite a steep climb and descent – to avoid this you could just retrace your steps from here back to the start of the walk.)

③ Turn left into a road alongside the Arethusa Venture Centre and where it bends left take the tarmac footpath ahead which goes uphill with houses on the left, then through trees. Where the path splits into three take the right hand path and follow it as it winds uphill through trees until you reach a minor road.

④ Turn left through a gateway to a parking area and along the top of a field past a seat, with fine views over the river to the Medway Towns and the North Downs beyond. Keep along the top of the field and at the far end turn right to another bench, through a gap in the hedge, and past a

The river Medway

playground on the right. On reaching a main road after 200 yards turn left for 100 yards to a narrow road on the left.

⑤ Go down this road, soon past a barrier, and continue for 400 yards until the road ends at a corrugated metal fence. Turn right here through a wooden gate and follow the path downhill, quite steep in places.

⑥ On reaching a T-junction with another path turn left and follow this path for 400 yards as it runs parallel to a road, to reach a road. Turn left for 100 yards to return to point 2. Turn right up the steps at the

footpath sign just past Normandie House on the right and follow the path back to Upper Upnor.

PLACES OF INTEREST NEARBY
Upnor Castle (English Heritage) is a riverside gun fort, built around 1600. Open daily April to October. Telephone: 01634 718742/ 827980.
World Naval Base, The Historic Dockyard, Chatham. 400 years of naval history, tours of ships and submarine. Open daily April to October, Wednesday, Saturday and Sunday in February, March and November. Telephone: 01634 823800.

Biddenden
The Red Lion

DIRECTIONS TO START: BIDDENDEN IS 5 MILES NORTH-WEST OF TENTERDEN, AT THE JUNCTION OF THE A274 FROM MAIDSTONE AND THE A262. THE INN IS IN THE CENTRE OF THE VILLAGE, ON THE A262, WITH THE PUBLIC CAR PARK AT THE JUNCTION OF THE TWO A ROADS. **PARKING:** IN THE PUBLIC CAR PARK, OR, WITH PERMISSION, IN THE CAR PARK BEHIND THE PUB, REACHED BY A ROAD FROM THE A274.

The lovely village of Biddenden has retained its medieval charm, despite the traffic going through it. There are many historical stories associated with the village and the surrounding area. One of these is depicted on the village sign – the legend of the two maids of Biddenden. These were twin sisters, born in 1100 joined at the shoulders and hips, who lived in this condition for 34 years. There is a large church, reflecting the past wealth of the area in the 15th century as a result of the cloth trade. Many of the houses in the village date from the 17th century, and are fine examples of Kentish timber-frame construction. The pavements are made of 'Bethersden marble', a local limestone. This stroll, completely off-road, goes through pleasant countryside to the north and west of the church.

The Red Lion

This pub was founded in the 17th century. There is a beam above the fireplace with the date 1694 carved in it, and a framed list of landlords through the years hangs on the wall. The original house is said to have been built by a soldier who returned from the battle of Agincourt in 1415. The beamed bars are tastefully furnished and comfortable, and there is a separate dining area. There are old agricultural implements on display, to add to the interest.

Beers served include Shepherd Neame Master Brew and Flowers and there are also Heineken and Stella Artois lagers, Scrumpy Jack cider, and Guinness on draught. Chicken Penang and beef curry are among the main dishes, as well as smoky American chicken, seafood parcel, salmon pasta, Portobello steak and chicken breast with apple, onions and mushrooms in a rich cider sauce. The opening times are 12 noon to 3 pm and 6 pm to 11 pm on Monday to Thursday and all day on Friday to Sunday, with food served from 12 noon to 2 pm and 7 pm to 9 pm. Telephone: 01580 291347.

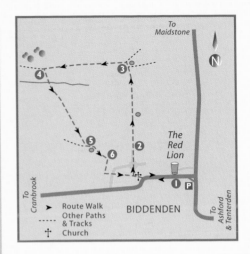

The Walk

NB: The route is fairly flat throughout, but there are several tall stiles.

① From the pub go towards the church, through the lychgate, and on the path to the right of the church. Part way through the churchyard take a path to the right, near a green lamppost. Go between fences, then straight across a patch of grass with trees, and at the end of the cul-de-sac ahead continue on a concrete path.

② Where the houses on the left end, go straight on and keep to the right edge of a meadow, and of the next three fields. Go past a large pond on the right and over a stile in the wire fence at the end of the field. Bear slightly left across the next field, aiming 25 yards left of a telegraph pole at the far end. Go through a gap in the hedge, over a plank bridge, and along the right edge of the next field to a smaller pond.

③ At the end of this pond turn sharp left along the top of this field and the next one to reach a stile. Notice the vineyard on the right here. Keep to the right across the next field, then in the next one look for a marker post in the hedge on the right.

④ Turn sharp left at this post and at the far end of the meadow go through a gap in the tall hedge to cross a stream, then diagonally left across a large field, aiming for the roofs of houses in the distance.

Biddenden village

This field is colourful with flowers and butterflies in summer.

⑤ At the far corner of the field go over a stile on the left, then along the right edge of a field for 50 yards. Immediately after a small pond on the right, go over a stile and diagonally across a small field, aiming for the church ahead.

⑥ After a stile turn left for a few yards, then go between metal barriers and straight down a road between houses. At the end of the road, by a parking area, turn left along a tarmac path and follow it back to the churchyard.

PLACES OF INTEREST NEARBY

At **Biddenden Vineyards and Cider Works** there are wines and ciders to sample, vineyard trails, a shop and a tearoom. Open daily throughout the year except for Sundays in January and February and 24 December to 1 January. Telephone: 01580 291726. **Sissinghurst Castle Garden** (National Trust), off the A262 west of Biddenden, is a world famous connoisseur's garden in the grounds of the remains of an Elizabethan mansion. Open daily except Mondays, April to mid-October. Telephone: 01580 710700.

Appledore
The Black Lion

MAP: OS EXPLORER 125 (GR 957293) — **WALK 20** — **DISTANCE:** 4½ MILES

DIRECTIONS TO START: APPLEDORE IS ON THE B2080, WHICH CAN BE TAKEN EAST FROM TENTERDEN OR WEST FROM THE A2070 AT BRENZETT. THE PUB IS AT THE SOUTH END OF THE MAIN VILLAGE STREET, NEXT TO THE CHURCH. THE PUBLIC CAR PARK IS ON THE RIGHT OF THE MAIN STREET, GOING SOUTH. **PARKING:** PARKING IN FRONT OF THE PUB IS VERY RESTRICTED, SO IT IS BETTER TO PARK IN THE PUBLIC CAR PARK, 400 YARDS TO THE NORTH, OFF THE MAIN STREET.

Romney Marsh has an atmosphere of its own, a slightly mysterious other-worldliness. It is a land of watery ditches and dykes, herds of sheep, and far-reaching views over the flat landscape. It also has tiny isolated churches and distinctive wildlife.

This walk is slightly longer than the others, but is mainly flat, and you may see herons, swans and possibly even a kingfisher. It starts in Appledore, a charming village, which in the distant past was a port used as a base by Vikings. The village was destroyed by French invaders in 1380, but was rebuilt, and some of the lovely houses lining the wide main street date back to the 15th century. The walk also goes alongside the Royal Military Canal, built in 1804–7 to prevent further French attacks by Napoleon's army.

The Black Lion

Standing next to the ancient church, the Black Lion is near the spot where a regular market was held for several centuries. The market has gone, but the inn still serves fine food and drink. There is a good choice of ales such as Hancocks HB, Bass, Greene King IPA and Level Best from the Rother Valley Brewing Co, as well as Grolsch, Carling and Stella Artois lagers, Woodpecker and Blackthorn ciders and Guinness and Caffrey's stouts. The food is served in comfortable and spacious bar areas, decorated with old jugs and bottles and old photographs of the village. There is an extensive choice of fresh fish dishes, featuring salmon, trout, lemon sole and sea bass amongst others, also a luxury fish pie. Local lamb is on offer too, plus steaks, pies, curries and pasta dishes, as well as vegetarian choices such as pasta, avocado and Stilton bake. Lighter snacks include sandwiches (not Sundays), ploughman's lunches, and jacket potatoes. There is outdoor seating in front of the pub, with a pleasant outlook over the village.

The pub is open from 11.30 am to 11 pm daily, with food available from 11.30 am until 9.45 pm. Telephone: 01233 758206.

The Walk

① From the public car park go south down the main street past the Black Lion and the church and straight on down a road to the left of Queens Arms house. After 150 yards, shortly before a bridge, go left at a Royal Military Canal Path fingerpost and

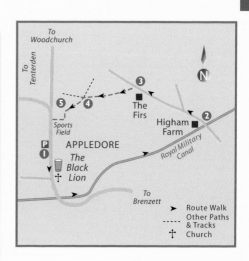

through a gate to the bank of the canal. Follow the bank, or the alternative path below it, for 2 miles. There is plenty of wildlife interest, with waterbirds, aquatic plants and colourful dragonflies. You will also see more recent defences against invasion, Second World War pillboxes.

② When you reach a narrow road near a farmhouse leave the canal and turn left along the road. Where it forks after ¼ mile take the left fork and continue for another ½ mile.

③ Just past a white house called The Firs go left over a stile signposted 'Saxon Shore Way', a long-distance path followed for the rest of the walk. Go diagonally right across a large field to a plank bridge, then straight across the next field and through a gap in the hedge. Continue straight across the next field, just to the left of the first telegraph pole. The path climbs gradually, with sweeping views over Romney Marsh to Dungeness power station and back to the North Downs in the far distance. Go straight on at a marker post at the far end

The Royal Military Canal near Appledore

of the field and along the right edge of the next field.

④ Where the line of trees on the right ends go diagonally left over a small mound with trees to a marker post, then straight down the field, under power lines, to a stile near two large oak trees. Continue straight on across a small field to a plank bridge hidden in the hedge in the far corner, then diagonally left across the next field towards houses.

⑤ At a marker post at the far side turn left along the field edge, then just past back gardens turn right through a metal gate and up a tarmac track to a road. Turn left along the road to return to the main part of the village.

> ### PLACES OF INTEREST NEARBY
> The **South of England Rare Breeds Centre** at Woodchurch, to the north of Appledore, has rare breeds of farm animals, tractor rides, a playground, a shop and a restaurant. Open daily (except Mondays from October to March). Telephone: 01233 861493.

Pluckley
The Black Horse

MAP: OS EXPLORER 137 (GR 926454)   **WALK 21**   **DISTANCE:** 2½ MILES

DIRECTIONS TO START: PLUCKLEY IS ON A MINOR ROAD, AND CAN BE REACHED BY GOING SOUTH FROM THE A20 AT CHARING OR NORTH FROM THE A28 AT BETHERSDEN. THE CAR PARK OF THE PUB IS OFF THE MAIN ROAD THROUGH THE VILLAGE BY THE SPORTS FIELD, ON THE LEFT SIDE WHEN TRAVELLING SOUTH. **PARKING:** THERE IS LIMITED PARKING IN FRONT OF THE PUB, BUT A LARGER CAR PARK BEHIND.

Pluckley is a small village in a lovely hillside setting. The beautiful and tranquil countryside in this area was made famous by the books of H. E. Bates, and particularly by their adaptation for the television series *The Darling Buds of May*. Much of the filming for the TV programmes was done in and around the village. For several centuries the land here was owned by the Dering family, who left their legacy in the unusual round-topped windows to be seen in many of the houses and the inn, the Black Horse. Legend has it that this shape was introduced because an ancestor of the family had evaded his enemies by escaping through a window of that shape. Other legends here involve things of another world, for Pluckley lays claim to being the most haunted village in England. About a dozen ghosts have been reported, including a highwayman. The walk goes through pleasant countryside and fruit orchards, with some lovely views.

The Black Horse

This ancient inn dates from the 15th century and is in the centre of the village, near the 13th century church. It contributes to the ghostly legends, by having a presence that is said to rearrange the furniture. There is plenty to move, as the spacious restaurant can seat 60 people beneath its beams and around the vast inglenook fireplace. There is also a bar area, decorated with old agricultural implements and photographs of stars of the *Darling Buds* TV series, and a large garden.

Several real ales are available, such as Rebellion Smuggler from Marlow, Flowers Original and Fuller's London Pride, as well as Stella Artois and Heineken lagers, Guinness and Caffrey's stouts and Strongbow cider on draught. There is also a good choice of food, ranging from snacks such as jacket potatoes, baguettes, ploughman's lunches and doorstep sandwiches through burgers, fish and chips or sausage and mash to full restaurant meals. Examples of these are steaks, mixed grill and stuffed saddle of rabbit, with daily specials such as tuna in a creamy lime sauce. Children's meals are also available.

The pub is open all day, every day. Food is available all day Monday to Saturday and at Sunday lunchtime, when roast meats are also served. Telephone: 01233 840256.

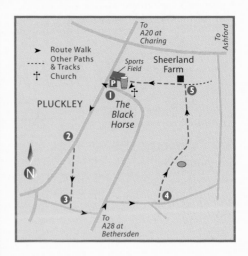

The Walk

① Turn right from the front of the pub, to soon reach a T-junction. Cross the road carefully and turn left on the path alongside the road. Follow it downhill, soon with a lovely thatched cottage on the left, then tremendous views on the right.

② After ¼ mile, just before a bend, cross the road with care at a footpath sign to a narrow path to the left of a domestic garage. After going between fences, the path continues across a field to stiles, then slightly left across a larger field to a stile in the far corner. Over this, keep straight on along the right edge of the next field to a minor road.

③ Turn left along the road for 400 yards to a T-junction, then go left again. After 300 yards turn right into a lane at the end of a row of houses (or continue on for a shortcut back to the village). Walk along this quiet lane for 600 yards, keeping left where it forks.

④ About 100 yards past the fork go left over a stile by a footpath sign, opposite a row of cottages. Keep to the right edge of two fields to a stile in the hedge in the right

The Weald, near Pluckley

corner. Continue straight ahead on a track between a windbreak hedge on the right and an orchard on the left. Follow this track, which may be muddy, for ¼ mile past more orchards until it reaches a tarmac farm road. Continue on this road, crossing another farm road, and carry on with a tall hedge on the right.

⑤ On reaching a cross track, shortly before some stone barns ahead, turn left. The wide track soon passes a large house with a formal rose garden, goes through a belt of trees, then continues between orchards. After ½ mile it reaches a sports field. Go left through the churchyard to the front of the pub, or continue to the end of the field to reach the car park.

PLACES OF INTEREST NEARBY

Godinton House and Gardens, just north-west of Ashford, has lovely gardens and trees surrounding a Jacobean house. Open mid-April to mid-October. Telephone: 01233 620773. **Dering Wood**, south-west of Pluckley, is a Woodland Trust nature reserve with interesting wildlife. Telephone: 01476 581135.

Newnham
The George

MAP: OS EXPLORER 149 (GR 954577)   **WALK 22**   DISTANCE: 3½ MILES

DIRECTIONS TO START: NEWNHAM IS REACHED BY MINOR ROADS RUNNING SOUTH FROM THE A2 WEST OF FAVERSHAM. THE PUB IS OPPOSITE THE CHURCH.
PARKING: IN THE PUB CAR PARK, WITH PERMISSION.

The countryside around Newnham, on the top of the North Downs, has lovely wooded hills and valleys, and it is not surprising that this is designated as an area of outstanding natural beauty. Much of the walk is on quiet lanes, so is mostly dry underfoot. It passes some interesting medieval houses, provides the opportunity to visit the colourful gardens at Doddington Place, and goes close to orchards of cherries, a fruit for which this region has long been famous.

The George

This welcoming inn has several bars, each with its own large fireplace, and a separate eating area. The menu includes delicacies such as Norfolk duck in a blackcurrant and port sauce, and sea bass with asparagus. There is also a good selection of lighter meals, including bangers and mash, fisherman's pie, pasta, pancakes and curries, as well as Sunday roasts. The tempting range of desserts features sticky toffee pudding, spotted dick, cheesecakes and profiteroles. Shepherd Neame beers on offer include Goldings, Bishop's Finger, Spitfire and Master Brew, and there are also lagers, ciders and an extensive wine list. On warm days you can sit in the pleasant large garden at the rear.

Opening times are 11 am to 3 pm and 6.30 pm to 11 pm, and food is served from 12 noon to 2 pm and 7 pm to 9 pm. Telephone: 01795 890237.

The Walk

① Cross the road at the front of the pub to Seed Road, which goes to the left of the church and soon between cherry orchards.

② After 1 mile, just before medieval Foxenden Manor, turn right up Hopes Hill Road and follow this for ¾ mile between trees and tall hedges, later with a good view across fields towards Doddington Place on the right.

③ On reaching Doddington village turn right for 50 yards, then left up a road past the Chequers pub, which has a good choice of beers and prize-winning local sausages.

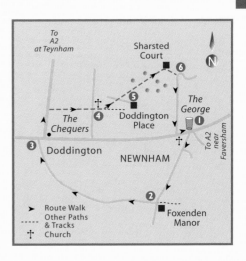

Take care walking along this busier road, and at the top of the hill look for a footpath going off between bungalows on the right. At the end of the gardens go straight across a field, then left for 20 yards before going right over a stile. Continue over another stile, across a small field, then left of a wire fence, with good views back to the right over Doddington and the surrounding countryside. Go over a stile in the right corner of the field to a minor road.

④ Go straight across the road to a drive and pass Doddington church on the left. Go through a metal gate, then diagonally left (not straight on) across a field with ancient parkland trees to a stile in a wire fence. Cross the drive of Doddington Place to another stile. (The tearooms at Doddington Place Gardens are open to non-visitors.)

⑤ Go diagonally right to enter a wood at its corner and where a wire fence on the right ends go straight on, not right. Keep straight on through the wood and over a stile next to a metal gate. Bear right on a

Sharsted Court, one of the medieval houses to be found near Newnham

track as it goes in front of the fine medieval Sharsted Court, with its impressive topiary. Take the left fork of the track once past the house to reach a minor road.

⑥ Turn right on this road to return to Newnham village, then turn left to return to the pub.

PLACES OF INTEREST NEARBY

Doddington Place Gardens has 10 acres of lovely landscaped grounds, including woodland and rock gardens. Open from Easter to September, Tuesday to Thursday and Sunday. Telephone: 01795 886101. **Belmont** to the east of Newnham and reached via Eastling, is a charming 18th century house with fine collections of clocks and furniture. Open at weekends between April and September. Telephone: 01795 890202.

Hernhill
The Red Lion

MAP: OS EXPLORER 149 (GR 065607)   **WALK 23**   **DISTANCE:** 2½ MILES

DIRECTIONS TO START: NEAR JUNCTION 7 OF THE M2, HERNHILL CAN BE REACHED ON MINOR ROADS, SOUTH FROM THE A299 OR NORTH FROM THE A2(T) AT BOUGHTON STREET. **PARKING:** IN THE CAR PARK BEHIND THE PUB, WITH PERMISSION.

The small village of Hernhill sits in some lovely gently-rolling countryside on the edge of what was once the vast forest of Blean. However, much of this woodland has been cleared over the centuries, except on the nearby hills. Instead, the village is now surrounded by orchards of apples, pears, cobnuts and cherries, and fields of strawberries, all seen on the walk. In spring the orchards are a glorious vision of white and pink blossom, while in autumn the leaves glow red and gold.

The Red Lion

In a picturesque setting next to the village green and opposite the lovely 11th century church, the Red Lion has occupied its position for a long time, the building dating from the 14th century. There is an extensive choice of excellent food and drink available, and meals can be taken in the spacious bar with its secluded alcoves, or in the restaurant upstairs. As you would expect in a building of this antiquity both are extensively beamed.

The à la carte menu includes fish dishes featuring monkfish, sea bass and salmon, and rack of lamb, guinea fowl and duck are among the meat dishes. There is also a varied bar menu, with beef braised in ale and onions, steak, mixed grill, and daily specials such as roast pheasant with red wine and mushroom sauce. Both menus have vegetarian choices and there are salads, ploughman's lunches, baguettes and jacket potatoes. Liquid refreshment is not neglected, with Boddingtons, Wadworth 6X and Shepherd Neame Master Brew available, plus Addlestone's cloudy cider and local apple juice. Outside there are seats overlooking the green at the front and a large garden has children's play equipment at one end.

The pub is open from 11.30 am to 3 pm and from 6 pm to 11 pm Monday to Saturday and from 12 noon to 3 pm and 7 pm to 10.30 pm on Sunday. Food is served from 12 noon to 2 pm and 6 pm (6.30 pm on Sunday) to 9.30 pm. Telephone: 01227 751207.

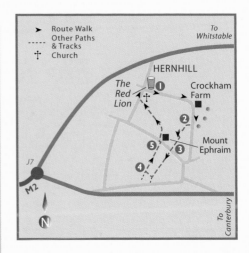

The Walk

① Leaving the front of the pub go left down a narrow lane running between houses, then past orchards and fields of strawberries. Keep straight on where another lane comes in from the left, with views back to Hernhill church on the right, and continue downhill.

② For the next section of the walk the paths are not well marked. On the left a wood comes right down to the road, and 50 yards past this point turn right off the lane through a gap in the hedge (no footpath sign) onto a grassy farm track. After 50 yards go left over a stile in the low wire fence and up a small field past a telegraph post to cross a stile in a line of tall poplars. Follow the poplars round an orchard by going right for 50 yards, then left for 70 yards. Where the poplars veer right go diagonally left through the orchard to a gap in an alder windbreak, then straight down through another orchard to another line of poplars. Turn right for 70 yards to a gap onto a road.

On the walk with Mount Ephraim House in the background

③ Cross the road to a private drive to The Bounds and keep on this drive past a converted oasthouse and straight on where another track crosses. Continue uphill, with views to Mount Ephraim house on the right. Just before the walls of a derelict building on the right, turn right on a path that goes between fences.

④ After 200 yards, at a T-junction with another path, turn right. This path continues between fences with orchards beyond, then with a row of tall horse chestnuts and a stream on the right, until it reaches a road.

⑤ Go left for 20 yards, then right through the gates of Mount Ephraim Gardens.

Keep straight on where the drive forks after 30 yards and then straight on past houses on the left. Continue on this tarmac drive, with Hernhill church seen ahead and lovely views to the right, to a road, then go right to return to the pub.

PLACES OF INTEREST NEARBY

Mount Ephraim Gardens: 8 acres of delightful Edwardian gardens. Open mid-April to mid-September (not Tuesdays and Fridays). Telephone: 01227 751496. At Nash Court, west of Boughton Street (near junction 7 of the M2), there are farm animals, birds of prey, an adventure playground, a museum and farm trails at **Farming World**. Open daily from March to November. Telephone: 01227 751144.

Chilham
The White Horse

DIRECTIONS TO START: CHILHAM IS AT THE JUNCTION OF THE A28 BETWEEN ASHFORD AND CANTERBURY AND THE A252. THE VILLAGE CAN BE REACHED FROM EITHER ROAD, AND THE PUB IS IN THE MAIN SQUARE. **PARKING:** IN THE PUBLIC CAR PARK, JUST OFF THE A252, OR IN THE VILLAGE SQUARE.

This walk is in a lovely part of Kent, where the river Stour cuts a gap through the chalk of the North Downs. As a bonus the village of Chilham has a well-deserved reputation of being one of the prettiest villages in the whole of England. Grouped around the village square are wonderful black and white timbered houses, with an ancient church at one end and a Jacobean mansion with adjacent Norman castle keep at the other. As if this weren't enough the walk also passes an ancient burial mound and a beautifully preserved water mill, and has tremendous views over the Stour valley.

The White Horse

Standing at one end of the village square, the White Horse does not look out of place in such an historical setting, as it has a long history of its own. It was built in the 15th century as a thatched cottage and later became the home of the church vicars. One of these, who died alone and penniless after being stripped of his office, is reputed to haunt the inn. Fortunately, the spirit seems to be benign, apparently preventing falling glasses from breaking. The bars provide a cosy ambience, and in one there is a large 15th century inglenook fireplace carved with pre-Tudor roses. Outside, there is a pleasant little garden.

The menu includes fish and chips, scampi and chips, cheese and chicken pasta, steak in red wine, and specials such as sweet and sour pork. Vegetable jambalaya and vegetable tikka masala are examples of the vegetarian meals available, whilst among the lighter snacks you will find doorstep sandwiches and jacket potatoes. Desserts include apple flan and chocolate fudge cake. There is a good range of ales, including Flowers, Young's and Fuller's London Pride, also Heineken lager, Murphy's stout and Scrumpy Jack cider.

Opening times are 11 am to 11 pm, with food served from 12.30 pm to 2.30 pm and 6.30 pm to 9 pm. Telephone: 01227 730355.

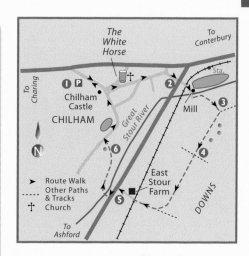

The Walk

① From the public car park turn right to the village square, with the inn opposite. From the corner of the square to the right of the church go down the road called The Street past lovely cottages and later the Woolpack inn. Continue straight on for another ¼ mile and follow the road as it bends right in front of houses to reach a main road opposite a service station.

② Cross with care to the minor road opposite, then over the railway, to soon pass a lovely white-boarded water mill on the left. Cross a river, then turn left along the riverbank for a short distance, then away from it through trees, across a track, then up the left edge of a field.

③ At the top of the field go through a gap in the trees, then turn immediately right on a track. This track, part of the Stour Valley Walk, goes between trees, with occasional views across the valley to Chilham church and castle.

④ After ½ mile the track splits into three by a marker post. Take the middle, grassy path straight ahead and follow it between hedges for ½ mile, then cross a stile and turn right on a stony track, going under

Chilham's lovingly preserved water mill

the railway and between houses to a main road.

⑤ Turn left along the road verge for 80 yards then cross to a wooden pedestrian gate. Cross a footbridge then bear diagonally right across a field to a hedge 50 yards ahead. Turn right along the hedge, with Chilham Castle visible ahead. After 300 yards cross a stile and keep to the left edge of the next field, but after 150 yards go left at a stile in the hedge. Go diagonally right across the field to a small wood.

⑥ Enter the wood at a rather overgrown gap under telephone wires, then soon between gardens to a minor road. Turn right and follow the road, with the grounds of the castle on the left, and where it forks go left up School Hill to return to the village square.

PLACES OF INTEREST NEARBY

Canterbury, only 6 miles east of Chilham, has many attractions, including the **Cathedral, Roman Museum** (01227 785575) and **Canterbury Heritage Centre** (01227 452747).

Wye
The Tickled Trout

DIRECTIONS TO START: SITUATED 3 MILES NORTH-EAST OF ASHFORD, WYE IS REACHED ON A MINOR ROAD FROM THE A28. THE PUB IS JUST PAST THE LEVEL CROSSING.
PARKING: IN THE PUB CAR PARK, WITH PERMISSION, OR THE PUBLIC CAR PARK OFF CHURCHFIELD WAY. WYE RAILWAY STATION IS NEXT TO THE PUB.

Wye is a large village, nestling in a lovely setting where the river Stour cuts a gap through the chalk hills of the North Downs. The village has a 12th century church, many fine Georgian buildings, and a long history as a seat of learning. A college was founded here in the 15th century by the Archbishop of Canterbury and later became an agricultural college.

Wye makes a fine centre for many attractive walks in the surrounding hills and valleys, and this short stroll provides an opportunity to view some of the lovely buildings in the village and to get a close view of the hills. The Downs in this area are home to rare butterflies and flowers, including several species of orchids, and a section is a National Nature Reserve.

The Tickled Trout

This old inn is in a lovely position next to the river Stour. In fact the large garden goes right down to the riverbank, and has its own resident ducks. From the garden you can see the original 17th century bridge over the river, under the modern one. The main building of the Tickled Trout dates from about 1650, and was originally a tannery, becoming an inn during the reign of Queen Victoria. There are roomy bars with more secluded alcoves and beams draped with dried hops. This is particularly apposite here, as many varieties of hops have been bred at Wye. There is also a tastefully-decorated, spacious eating area in a conservatory on the side of the pub overlooking the river.

The menu includes sea bass, crab salad, fisherman's pie, trout, steaks, and shoulder of lamb. Lighter meals such as jacket potatoes and filled baguettes are available too. A good range of ales is on offer, such as Greene King IPA and Abbot, Caledonian Champion, Wychwood Hobgoblin and Young's Waggle Dance. Lagers, Guinness and Strongbow and Scrumpy Jack ciders are also on tap, and wines are available by the glass.

Opening times are 11 am to 2.30 pm and 6 pm to 11 pm (7 pm to 11 pm on Sunday), with food available from 12 noon to 2 pm and 6.30 pm to 9 pm. Telephone: 01233 812227.

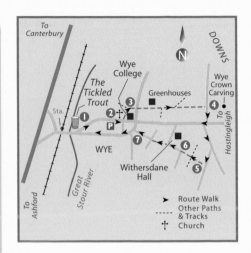

The Walk

① From the front of the pub turn left and after 30 yards turn left up Churchfield Way and follow it to the village church (passing the public car park). To view the oldest part of the college continue for another 100 yards to see it on the left, then return to the entrance to the churchyard.

② Take the footpath that goes diagonally across the churchyard to the right of the church, then go left on a footpath that soon turns right to a road.

③ Go straight across to the minor road opposite and keep on past university experimental greenhouses on the left. Where the road ends continue along the tree-lined stony track as it goes gradually uphill with fine views to the Downs ahead and to the left. Ignore any paths going off to the sides.

④ When the track reaches a minor road turn right, with views left to the crown carved in the chalk by Wye students to commemorate the coronation of Edward VII in 1902. At a junction with another road, go up Amage Road opposite, then after 250 yards go down a lane between houses on the right, signposted 'Dairy Farm'.

Looking towards the Downs

⑤ After 400 yards go over a stile on the right to a farm track and follow it between fields, with more lovely views to the hills on the right, then past a hop garden on the right behind the shelter of a tall beech hedge.

⑥ On reaching a minor road go straight ahead for 100 yards, with views of Withersdane Hall, now part of the University, on the right, then where the road bends right go straight ahead down a track. The track runs alongside a beech hedge on the left until it reaches another minor road. Go straight across to another path which soon becomes a narrow road between houses.

⑦ When you reach a main road turn left and follow it through the village back to the pub, or turn right after 200 yards then left at the church to return to the public car park.

> ### PLACES OF INTEREST NEARBY
> **Wye National Nature Reserve**, off the road to Hastingleigh, south-east of Wye, has many rare wildflowers, including orchids, and butterflies, plus lovely views. It is managed by English Nature. Telephone: 01233 812525.

Lympne
The County Members

MAP: OS EXPLORER 138 (GR 119349) **WALK 26** **DISTANCE:** 2¾ MILES

DIRECTIONS TO START: FROM JUNCTION 11 OF THE M20 GO WEST ON THE A20 (T) FOR 1 MILE TO NEWINGREEN, THEN SOUTH ON A MINOR ROAD TO LYMPNE. TURN RIGHT AT THE T-JUNCTION AFTER 1 MILE TO SOON REACH THE PUB ON THE LEFT. **PARKING:** IN THE PUB CAR PARK, WITH PERMISSION OR IN THE PUBLIC CAR PARK IN LYMPNE (GR 120349).

This walk is in an area steeped in history, going past the remains of a Roman fort, and with views of an ancient church and fortified manor house. The path goes along the former coastline and has fantastic views across Romney Marsh to the coast, and even to France on a clear day. Another section takes you along the bank of the Royal Military Canal, built in Napoleonic times to guard against invasion. As well as admiring the local flora and fauna you may see or hear more exotic animals as you walk beside fields belonging to the Port Lympne Wild Animal Park.

The County Members

This inn has roomy bars, a separate conservatory-style eating area, and a pleasant little garden. As befits a pub that is just a short distance from the coast, fish dishes feature prominently on the menu, with a luxury fish pie and specials such as sea bass in white wine sauce and skate wing. Meat dishes include steaks, duck in Grand Marnier and blackcurrant cassis sauce, and rack of lamb. Vegetarians are catered for with a Brie and redcurrant tart or, perhaps, creamy penne pasta with garlic roasted vegetables. If you have completed the walk and have worked up an appetite for a filling dessert you can choose from spotted dick and apple or pecan pies. Lighter snacks include sandwiches and baguettes. There is a good choice of ales, including Harveys, Flowers, Greene King IPA and Fuller's London Pride. Murphy's stout, lagers and ciders are also available.

Opening times are 11 am to 11 pm Monday to Saturday, and 12 noon to 10.30 pm on Sunday. Food is served from 12 noon to 2.30 pm and 7 pm to 9.30 pm on Monday to Saturday and from 12 noon to 9 pm on Sunday. Telephone: 01303 264759.

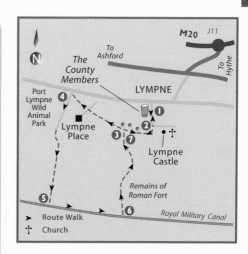

The Walk

① Turn right from the front of the pub, then immediately right down The Street, signposted to Lympne Castle.

② Where the road bends left go straight on at the footpath sign, down a track with cottages on the right. (It is worth a short diversion before you go down the track. Continue for 100 yards along the road to view the ancient church and castle, then retrace your steps.) Continue on the track through trees, then with a wood on the right and fine views on the left over Romney Marsh to the coast.

③ Go straight on at a marker post after 300 yards and continue for ½ mile on this path, part of the Saxon Shore Way (SSW) long-distance path and here following the old coastline. It crosses two private roads and goes through trees before emerging at the junction of a lane with a main road.

④ Turn sharp left here down the lane, later becoming a stony track, then a path. You are soon walking between tall fences surrounding compounds of a wild animal park, with glimpses of some of the animals. Your descent of the old coastline concludes as you go over a plank bridge to a raised bank.

⑤ This is the bank of the Royal Military Canal, seen through trees. Turn left at the

The view across Romney Marsh to the coast

marker post and walk along the bank for about ½ mile, passing a Second World War pillbox on the way.

⑥ At another post with SSW marker go left down the bank, with a view of Lympne Castle through a gap in the trees, to cross a plank bridge over a stream. The path then winds gradually uphill. The ruined stone walls in the field on the right are the remains of a Roman fort. The path is rather uneven in places so take care, and there are some steps.

⑦ On reaching a junction with another path by a wood turn right and keep to this path to return to point 2. Walk up the road ahead to return to the pub.

> **PLACES OF INTEREST NEARBY**
> **Port Lympne Wild Animal Park**. See gorillas, elephants, rhinos, tigers and lions in the grounds of an historic mansion. Open daily. Telephone: 09068 800605.

Elham
The King's Arms

MAP: OS EXPLORER 138 (GR 177438)   **WALK 27**   **DISTANCE:** 2½ OR 3 MILES

DIRECTIONS TO START: FROM JUNCTION 12 OF THE M20 GO WEST ON THE A20 (T) THEN NORTH ON A MINOR ROAD THROUGH LYMINGE. ONCE IN ELHAM, TURN EASTWARDS INTO THE VILLAGE SQUARE.
PARKING: IN THE SQUARE IN FRONT OF THE PUB.

Elham is a delightful village, set in a valley in the gently rolling countryside of the North Downs. The village has several historic buildings, including a 13th century church and a large Tudor house, now a restaurant. There are also three old inns to choose from, and gift, antique and book shops.

Surrounded by lovely countryside, Elham forms a fine centre for walks, though most of them, including the longer route described here, do involve some fairly steep climbs. However, the reward is superb views over the valley.

The King's Arms

This 400 year old hostelry stands in a superb setting in the historic village square, opposite the lovely church. It provides a fine range of food and drink, served in a friendly manner in the cosy bar or comfortable dining area. The menu includes a selection of fish dishes, including salmon, trout and lemon sole, as well as steaks, gammon, pies, curry and chilli con carne. There is also a choice of vegetarian meals, such as aubergine, tomato and mozzarella layer. In addition, there are Sunday roasts and lighter snacks like sandwiches, baguettes, ploughman's lunches and jacket potatoes. A good choice of ales is on offer, featuring bitters by such brewers as Harveys, Brakspear and Flowers, as well as lagers, ciders, stouts and an extensive wine list.

The pub is open from 11 am to 3 pm and 6 pm to 11 pm, with food available from 12 noon to 2 pm and 6 pm to 9 pm (except Sunday evening). Telephone: 01303 840242.

The Walk

① From the front of the inn cross the village square, admiring the fine buildings around it, then turn left down Duck Street, next to the church. Go past houses, then continue on as the lane narrows and climbs gradually between ancient hedges.

② Where the lane bends left, climb up the bank on the right, past a bridleway sign. (*For the shorter walk*, avoiding a steep climb, continue along the lane for ½ mile, to rejoin the route by going left at point 4.)

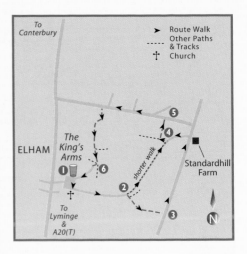

Go over a stile at the top of the bank and straight up a steep field. Pause from your exertions at the top to look back for a fantastic view over the village and the Elham valley. Continue over a stile and cross another field to the left corner of a fence, then keep straight on with a fence to your right, and over two more stiles to a minor road.

③ Turn left along the road for ½ mile then left along a lane opposite Standardhill Farm.

④ Where the lane bends left go straight on through a metal gate at a footpath sign. Keep to the right edge of the field and after 100 yards go over a stile on the right. Follow the left edge of a field, with lovely views to the left, to a minor road.

⑤ Turn left down the road, between tall hedges. Just before the first house on the left, go left at a stile in the hedge. This is part of the Elham Valley Way between Canterbury and Hythe. Keep to the right edge of a field, then the path bends right

Elham

and left as it follows the right edge of the next field. There are now tall poplars and a stream on the right, and you are following the route of the old Elham Valley Railway, now invisible.

⑥ Just before the village go through a metal gate on the right, over the stream, and diagonally left across a small field,

aiming for the church. Go through another gate and up a narrow lane past houses to return to the village square.

> **PLACES OF INTEREST NEARBY**
> **Elham Valley Vineyard** is at Breach, 3 miles north of Elham. There are wines to sample, plus a pottery and craft shop. Telephone: 01227 831266.

Littlebourne
The King William IV

| MAP: OS EXPLORER 150 (GR 210574) | WALK 28 | DISTANCE: 3¼ MILES |

DIRECTIONS TO START: LITTLEBOURNE IS 4 MILES EAST OF CANTERBURY,
ON THE A257. THE PUB IS AT THE EAST END OF THE VILLAGE.
PARKING: IN THE CAR PARK AT THE PUB, WITH PERMISSION.

This walk is in a flat area to the east of Canterbury and has wide vistas. It also has the attraction of passing through some lovely villages with old churches, built in a variety of styles, thatched cottages and impressive white-boarded water mills. There are also several pubs en route, so the temptation is to spend more time drinking than walking! Littlebourne itself sprawls along a main road, but just off the road are some fine buildings.

The King William IV

This traditional pub dates from 1790. It is a free house serving Bass and Shepherd Neame Master Brew beers and several lagers including Foster's, Heineken and Stella Artois. A range of wines is available by the glass. The menu changes regularly but examples of the superb meals on offer are lamb steak marinated in garlic, lemon and mint with Moroccan couscous and vegetarian choices such as roasted vegetable, pepper and goat's cheese strudel. The daily specials are mainly delicious fish dishes, for example whole sea bass with a basil, pine nut and lemon sauce. Among the lighter meals are nachos, steak and ale pie, and mussels in white wine, as well as sandwiches, baguettes, ploughman's lunches and jacket potatoes. The very tempting desserts include raspberry and almond torte with white chocolate sauce and coffee and walnut roulade with butterscotch sauce. All this is served in a pleasant eating area, decorated with horse brasses on the beams and old photographs of the village.

The pub is open from 11 am to 11 pm, with food served from 12 noon to 2.30 pm and 7 pm to 9.30 pm. Telephone: 01227 721244.

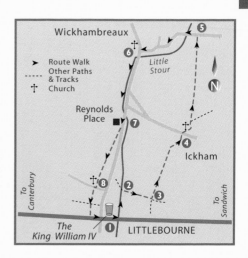

The Walk

① Turn left from the pub alongside the main road. Immediately after crossing the river turn left to follow a track, with glimpses of the river through the yew hedge on the left.

② Near a house on the left, take a hidden path on the right, by a marker post. Go past a shed, across a field to the right edge of a row of trees, then across another field to a track near a house.

③ Turn sharp left on the track and follow it, with views of a church and oast houses ahead, for ½ mile, then go diagonally right across a field to the left side of the oast houses and continue to a road. This is the lovely village of Ickham, with historic buildings and another good pub.

④ Turn right for 30 yards then left to the church. Go right of the churchyard and round it to a track. Follow this for ½ mile between fields of cereals and vegetables, with far-reaching views.

⑤ At a minor road turn left to cross the Little Stour river and continue to a T-junction by a thatched cottage. Turn left to Wickhambreaux village green, bordered by the church, a water mill and another pub.

Ickham village visited on the walk

⑥ Cross the green towards the church, but go left at a metal gate and through the churchyard to a gap in a wall, then along the left edge of a large field. Where the stream on the left veers off left keep straight on and continue behind gardens to a road by another white mill house.

⑦ Turn right along the road for 50 yards past Reynolds Place then go right at a stile into a small field. Keep to the left edge to reach a path between a garden and a hedge, then cross a field to Littlebourne church. Go to the left of the church to a road.

⑧ Turn right for 50 yards to an alley opposite, just before a school, and follow it past houses to a recreation ground and continue along the left edge to a main road. Turn left to return to the pub.

PLACES OF INTEREST NEARBY

Wingham Wildlife Park, along the A257 to the east, has a wide variety of animals, including monkeys, llamas, wallabies and meerkats, plus many different birds and an adventure playground. Open daily. Telephone: 01227 722053.

Howletts Wild Animal Park at Bekesbourne has the largest captive gorilla group in the world, plus tigers, elephants and many other animals. Open daily. Telephone: 09068 800605.

Sarre
The Crown

MAP: OS EXPLORER 150 (GR 257650)   **WALK 29**   **DISTANCE:** 2¾ MILES

DIRECTIONS TO START: SARRE IS BETWEEN CANTERBURY AND RAMSGATE, WITH THE PUB ON THE NORTH SIDE OF THE A253, JUST EAST OF ITS JUNCTION WITH THE A28.
PARKING: IN THE CAR PARK BEHIND THE PUB, WITH PERMISSION.

The small village of Sarre used to be an important port before the wide waterway that divided the Isle of Thanet from the rest of Kent became silted up. It is only 3 miles from the coast, and sea breezes blow across the flat landscape, which provides extensive views. The surrounding area, once marshland, has been drained, and now provides fertile soil for farming.

This stroll is on level ground, with a good surface underfoot for the most part, and with no stiles to negotiate. It passes through the historic village of St Nicholas at Wade, and you can also view a windmill that has been restored to working order.

The Crown

The inn has a long history, dating back to the 16th century, as evidenced by the 'priest's hole' found in the roof space. There is also a friendly mop-capped ghost. However, the spirit for which the inn is most famous is cherry brandy, made to a secret recipe brought over by the Huguenots, and only sold here. You will follow famous characters such as Charles Dickens, Rudyard Kipling and Douglas Fairbanks by sampling it. There is also a fine range of food and drink on offer, all served in a friendly atmosphere in the comfortable bars and pleasant restaurant area. On fine days you can sit in the attractive little garden.

Examples of the restaurant menu are deep-fried Camembert and oriental crab cakes as starters, while main meals include Guinea fowl, venison, sea bass, Thai pork fillet and roasted vegetable galette, followed by desserts such as apple strudel or crêpe suzette. Among the daily specials you could find smoked trout with tagliatelle and chargrilled barracuda. Bar meals include sausages and mash, steak and kidney pie, and mussels, while sandwiches, ploughman's lunches and jacket potatoes are also available. Shepherd Neame Master Brew and Spitfire bitters, Oranjeboom lager and ciders provide liquid refreshment.

Opening times are 11 am to 11 pm, with food served from 12 noon to 2.30 pm and 7 pm to 9.30 pm. Telephone: 01843 847808.

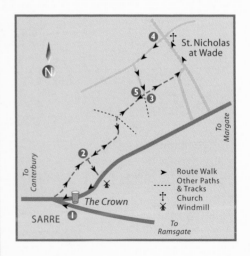

The Walk

① Leaving the front of the inn, turn right to a road junction and cross the main road ahead. Opposite is a flagpole, and a path by a post with a Wantsum Way marker. Go to the right of a white house then take a path on the right, opposite the side of this house. The path goes between hedges, then along the right edge of a field, with a hedge on the right.

② At the end of the hedge keep straight on between fields, then between hedges, colourful with berries and hips in autumn, to a metal gate. After the gate go straight ahead between fields towards a church and houses in the distance.

③ The path goes past houses on the left, along the right edge of a sports field, then between hedges to a road. Turn left for 30 yards to a T-junction near the village forge. Turn left to walk through the village of St Nicholas at Wade, with many fine old buildings, some with Dutch gables. You also pass (or fail to) two more pubs.

Sarre windmill

④ Opposite the magnificent 14th century tower of the church, which has for centuries been a landmark for shipping, turn left along Down Barton Road. Where the houses on the right end, turn left down Summer Road to return to point 3, where the bungalows on the left end.

⑤ Retrace your steps from this point by turning right on the path between fields, through the metal gate, and between hedges then fields until you reach the corner of the wood near the windmill. Turn left here for 100 yards to the main road. The windmill has a tearoom if you require further refreshment. Turn right on the path alongside the main road and you will soon see the car park of the inn on the left.

> **PLACES OF INTEREST NEARBY**
> **Sarre Mill** is a working windmill, built in 1820, with a bakery, tearoom, farmyard animals and vintage machinery. Open daily (except Mondays from November to March). Telephone: 01843 847573.

St Margaret's at Cliffe
The Smugglers

MAP: OS EXPLORER 138 (GR 358447)   **WALK 30**   **DISTANCE:** 3 MILES (1 MILE FOR SHORT WALK)

DIRECTIONS TO START: ST MARGARET'S AT CLIFFE IS 3 MILES NORTH OF DOVER AND REACHED BY MINOR ROADS GOING EAST FROM THE A258. THE PUBLIC CAR PARK IS JUST SOUTH OF THE CHURCH, WITH THE SMUGGLERS OPPOSITE THE CHURCH.
PARKING: IN THE PUBLIC CAR PARK.

This walk provides the opportunity to get some bracing sea air, whilst taking in some glorious views of the white cliffs of Dover and over the English Channel to France. You can also watch the ferries and other ships steaming in and out of Dover harbour, and the cliffs that you stroll along on the full route are colourful with wild flowers and butterflies in the summer months. St Margaret's at Cliffe is slightly inland, but it is only a short distance to the beach at St Margaret's Bay.

The Smugglers

Although St Margaret's is a small village, there are no less than four pubs to choose from. The Smugglers has a modest frontage, but inside the bar is cosy and full of character and at the rear there is a pleasant dining area in a conservatory and a courtyard with further seating. The menu provides a good choice of food, with a range of Mexican dishes such as burritos, fajitas and chicken diablo. There are also pizzas with a variety of toppings, steak and salmon dishes, and vegetarian options such as mushroom stroganoff. Lemon sole Bretonne and pheasant with port and chestnut sauce are examples of the daily specials. Lighter meals include salads, baguettes, ploughman's lunches, tapas and nachos, and moules. There is a varied selection of ales, with Greene King IPA, Theakston, John Smith's and Gales HSB on offer, in addition to Scrumpy Jack cider and a wide range of lagers and wines.

Opening times are 12 noon to 3 pm and 5 pm to 11 pm, with food served from 12 noon to 1.45 pm and 6.30 pm to 9.45 pm (7 pm to 9.30 pm on Sunday). Telephone: 01304 853404.

The Walk

① From the public car park walk to the main street through the village near to the Norman church, with the Smugglers opposite, and turn right. Go past the Hope inn and turn left into Chapel Lane. Where the lane swings left go off right, down Droveway Gardens. Follow the concrete track as it bends right past houses, then

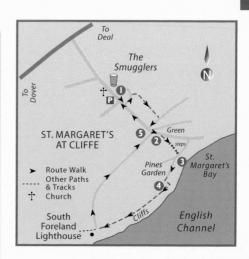

between fields and houses, to a road. Turn right for 100 yards to another road then left for a short distance to a large grassy area with fine views to the sea.

The next part of the walk is more strenuous, involving a long flight of descending steps, so if you want to return to the start from here go back straight up the road behind you.

② To continue the longer walk take the path that runs alongside the road going downhill to the right of the green. This path soon goes down steps to eventually reach a road. To visit the beach go straight on here, but the walk goes right at the Saxon Shore Way sign. Where the road forks after a short distance take the left fork.

③ Go past The Pines Garden on your right and as the road becomes a track follow it as it bends left then right on to the top of chalk cliffs. On your left are wonderful views over the English Channel and back over St Margaret's Bay.

The white cliffs at St Margaret's Bay

④ Continue on this track for ³/₄ mile, then shortly before the South Foreland lighthouse follow it as it bends right. Go through a gate to the left of a cattle grid ahead (ignoring another grid to the right). Follow the stony road as it continues past small grassy car parks and turns back to run parallel to the cliffs you have just traversed, but at a higher level. After ¹/₂ mile you pass another cattle grid, then the road widens out between houses.

⑤ The road ends at the grassy area at the top of Bay Hill. Turn left here to walk alongside the road back to the village.

> **PLACES OF INTEREST NEARBY**
> The **Pines Garden** is a peaceful 6-acre garden with a large lake and many fine trees and shrubs. Open daily. Telephone: 01304 852764. In nearby Dover there are several attractions such as **Dover Castle** (English Heritage, open daily, telephone: 01304 211067) and the **Museum** (open daily, telephone: 01304 201066).